*To Cheryl*

*James R. Knight* (signature)

# Letters to Anna

### The Civil War
*Through the Eyes and Heart of a Soldier*

# James R. Knight

Cold Tree Press
Nashville, Tennessee

Published by Cold Tree Press
Nashville, Tennessee
www.coldtreepress.com

Printed in the United States of America
ISBN 978-1-58385-170-8

# Table of Contents

Foreword                                                                i

CHAPTER 1    Birth of a Nation                                          1

CHAPTER 2    The Farmer and the President                              5

CHAPTER 3    Gone for Soldiers                                          9

CHAPTER 4    Confederate Forces—Unified Command                        13

CHAPTER 5    Union Forces—Divided Command                              19

CHAPTER 6    Union Forces—War and Politics                             25

CHAPTER 7    The Professional and the Politician                       29

CHAPTER 8    Two Rivers                                                 37

CHAPTER 9    Retreat and Regroup                                        49

CHAPTER 10   Shiloh                                                     53

CHAPTER 11   Northern Mississippi                                    57

CHAPTER 12   Back Home in Maury County                               65

CHAPTER 13   One Too Many Buggy Rides                                77

CHAPTER 14   Breaking the Stalemate                                  81

CHAPTER 15   The Lighting Brigade                                    85

CHAPTER 16   Captured—*"My fine mare went up when I did..."*         89

CHAPTER 17   Prisoner of War                                         93

CHAPTER 18   Johnson's Island                                        97

CHAPTER 19   *"Fresh Fish!"*                                        103

CHAPTER 20   Life in the Bull Pen                                   111

CHAPTER 21   Winter on Lake Erie                                    123

CHAPTER 22   False Hope                                             129

CHAPTER 23   Point Lookout                                          135

CHAPTER 24   Fort Delaware—*"I hope it will not prove to be any
             worse than Point Lookout got to be."*                  147

CHAPTER 25     Settling in for the Duration—*I am willing to endure almost anything for my country...*"                        155

CHAPTER 26     The Second Winter—*"Cold and inhospitable winter is coming Upon us with long strids..."*                        167

CHAPTER 27     Battles Close To Home—*"If we are to die, let us die like men..."*—Maj. Gen. Patrick Cleburne                    175

CHAPTER 28     *"Sturn Reality"*                                                                                               181

CHAPTER 29     Going Home—*"I have dispaired of our success for the first time since the war commenced."*                       189

CHAPTER 30     The Move West—*"To the Church at Alma Arkansas or elsewhere."*                                                   199

CHAPTER 31     Epilog—*"...he is a nice old gentleman, worthy of your consideration."*                                          209

About the Author                                                                                                               217

Bibliography                                                                                                                   219

Acknowledgments                                                                                                                223

# *Introduction*

The stories of hundreds of Civil War soldiers—great and small—have been told, and more are being discovered all the time. This story, like almost all those stories, is about a common man caught up in uncommon circumstances. One of the amazing things about this war and, I suppose, all wars, is the fact that so many men can endure the profound changes that war and combat bring, and then, when it's over, go back to being what they were before. In Burton Warfield's case, that was a husband, father, farmer, schoolteacher, church and community leader, and devoted son to his widowed mother.

Burton Warfield was thirty-two years old in 1861. The son of a cabinetmaker, he farmed a piece of ground near Hampshire, Tennessee, a few miles west of Columbia, where he was born. Like thousands of others, he left his young wife in charge of the farm, their children, and his widowed mother, and went to serve his new country.

———

*"[H]ad the pleasure of seeing a few Yankees and hear the balls from their minnie muskits whistle over our heads and among our feet ... I shot six times at them ... We captured about seven hundred Yankies and a good many negros ... A Yankey is a great curiosity to some of the boys. They are bad looking fellows generally ... They may over run us and despoil us of our homes, but from every hill top and from every secluded*

*spot the missils of death will be sent into their ranks from a foe they can never overcome ... conquer us they never can."*

—∞—

Burton Warfield was an educated and literate man—at least by the standards of the day. During his four years in Confederate service, Burton wrote many letters home. Some have been lost, but the Warfield family has preserved a large group. Somehow, in all his travels, Burton also managed to save several of his wife Anna's letters which he received in the field. A few have been published before, but most have not. The letters will be seen together here, in chronological order, for the first time. There are also a few letters from relatives and others which figure in the story, as well. The spelling and wording, including mistakes, from the original letters remain intact in the transcription, as penned by Burton and the other letter writers.

The letters cover the entire spectrum from patriotic pronouncements worthy of the best government propagandist to the everyday details of maintaining a household and farm in the middle of the storm of civil war.

—∞—

*"[W]hen I see the desolation of the fertile fields and fine estates of the people of Kentucky, and to see the women and gray headed sires fleeing from the oppression and insults of the invaders of these once happy homes is enough to excite the patriotism of every brave son of Tennessee to keep the same scenes of desolation and destruction from being enacted upon their own soil and their own homes ... How are you getting along farming? What is the prospect for fruit this year? ... Have you commenced plowing yet, got the fences all repaired?"*

—∞—

These letters also give little glimpses into the heart and character of the husband and wife. At various times, they each show impatience, frustration, anger, disillusionment, loneliness, strength, self-sacrifice, hope, faith, trust, humor, joy, and patriotism. Anna, although in enemy territory and with two small children and her mother-in-law to support, still tries several times to send Burton the money and clothing which are vital to his survival. She also gives the local, family, and church news along with occasional commentary on what she sees as the general decline in the moral standards that have come with the war and Yankee occupation.

For his part, Burton writes to assure Anna that he is well and confident in the righteousness of the "Cause," while sparing her and his mother the gory details of combat and some of the day-to-day realities of his situation. He sometimes tries, in his nineteenth-century Victorian style, to add a little humor while living in an environment which is beyond anything in his or Anna's previous experience, and at times, truly defies description.

—⟋⟍⟍—

*"We should bear the hardships and inconveniences of camp life with out a murmur while we know that our friends at home, and those we hold most dear, are secure from the desolating tread of an army much like that of an invading foe ... I know not whether I have a friend in Tenn. Are they friends, who, in your prosperity come to you with sweet smiles and flatering words, but in your adversity are as cold and silent as the grave? ... Is it because I am a rebel? Is it because I am a trator? Or is [it] because they are so devoted to Lincoln in the prosecution of this unholy war that they treat as enemies those they once hailed as friends. Is it so? God forbid ... We have quite a jolly crowd here [Yankee prison]. All kinds of amusements from a Thespian society, to ball and marble playing ... We have preaching here three or four times a week, lectures, debating societies, Bible classes. I belong to a bible class."*

—∞—

Around these letters, which sometimes leave considerable gaps in time, I will try to tell the story of Burton's war—not a detailed study of the war or of any campaign or battle, just the war as one man chanced to see it. His experiences, however, were shared by untold thousands of others in both Blue and Butternut. This, then, is the story of a schoolteacher and farmer turned Confederate Cavalry officer. He was one of many who fought for what they thought was right, kept the faith until all hope was lost, and then went home and put their lives back together. The history is woven in so as to show his place in the larger scheme of the war, but the story is Burton's—in his own words as much as possible.

—∞—

*"We lie down to rest at night to visit perhaps the beautiful and magic world of dreamland, which mocks us with its unattainable witcheries. We rise in the morning to behold the beaming rays of the sun as he rises as it were from the lake with its sparkling beauty. Sometimes as calm and placid as the bosom of the sleeping infant, not a breeze disturbs its smooth and limpid surface, then again foaming and surging in boisterous fury as if in its rage it would submerge our island home."*

—∞—

If you are expecting exciting details of combat or gruesome descriptions of battlefields or prison compounds in Burton's letters, you will be disappointed. Burton was writing to his young wife and aged mother who both feared for his safety. As a modest, Christian man of the Victorian era, he spared them much of the real story. Those gory details are left for me to provide.

Although Burton and his unit were in several engagements, only a few letters give personal details of any action. The letters concentrate much more on his health, the condition of his clothes, problems with his horse, the quality of his rations (or lack of same), the weather, the latest rumors, and, most of all, he asks about conditions at home. *How are the crops? What about family and friends and neighbors?* Also, over and over, there is the age-old soldier's complaint: *Why don't I get more mail?*

—⁓—

*"I am indeed verry anxious to hear from you and can't imagine why I do not get letters from home. Others here get letters regularly from Columbia. I trust you have not all forgotten me."*

—⁓—

Burton Warfield served the Confederacy from the spring of 1861 until the summer of 1865. From the beginning to the end, Burton rode, he fought, he froze, he starved, he praised the "Cause" and his fellow soldiers, he griped about shirkers at home, he worried about his horse, and he endured unspeakable conditions in four Yankee prisons. This soldier's letters serve to define an ordinary man placed in the extraordinary time of civil war—a man who experienced combat, captivity, and crushing defeat, and then went back home and got on with his life as best he could.

—⁓—

*"A gloom of sadness overspreads us at present. Gen Lee, the greatest and best man of the age, has surrendered … Our fond hopes of independence are all most crushed out. The great cause for which we have been strugling for four years to be abandoned and ourselves humiliated. I have nothing to regret … still believe that we were in the right."*

Fort Delaware, April 11th 1865

My Dear Anna.

Have you forgotten me, or what is the cause of your scilence? I write to you regularly but no answer or word from you. A gloom of sadness overspreads us at present. I have despaired of our success for the first time since the war commenced. Gen Lee the greatest and best man of the age has surrendered. The Army of Tenn now under Gen. Johnston will have to surrender if it has not already done so. What is to be done with us I know not. I hope to see you soon. in the mean time write to me. I would write you a longer letter but I fear you do not get my letters. My health is not as good as it has been. Nothing more than a cold though. Give my love to all, write soon.

Yours as ever.

Burton.

*Copy of original letter of Burton Warfield, dated April 11, 1865*

# Letters to Anna

## The Civil War
### Through the Eyes and Heart of a Soldier

# James R. Knight

CHAPTER ONE
## *Birth of a Nation*

*T*he year 1861 was like no other in the short history of the United States. It was to be the country's seventy-second year under the Constitution of 1789, but that centerpiece of the American experiment now seemed in danger of unraveling. While there were a few old folks who could still remember when the Constitution was ratified, for most Americans, the government it had brought into being was all they had ever experienced. Now that government, indeed the very existence of the United States as they knew it, was endangered. At the beginning of 1861, the country stood on the brink of civil war.

The United States was a grand experiment. There had never been anything quite like it in the world. Against overwhelming odds, the colonial rabble had won their independence from England, the superpower of the eighteenth century, and gained the right to govern themselves. The men we now call the Founding Fathers had to make up a framework for a new kind of nation. Many of the old rules represented the things they had rebelled against, but some of the new—some say radical— ideas might not work any better. No one knew for sure. After a false start with the Articles of Confederation, several years of trial and error, discussion and dispute, academic discourse, and plain old back-room politics finally produced the compromise document that became the United States Constitution and the first ten amendments, known as the Bill of Rights. It was to set the standard for representative government, a system that Winston Churchill was to call, in exasperation, years later, "the worst form of government known to man, except for all the others."

Fortunately for the new country, the theory of government set forth in the Constitution had proven sound, practical, and, on the whole, workable, but there were still problems to be solved and theories that hadn't been tested in practice or in the courts. One of these was the question of the extent of the rights reserved to the individual states. Many people, especially in the South, believed that "States' Rights" extended even to the right to withdraw from the Union if a majority of the people in that state wished it. This was called "Secession," and it had been discussed and debated for many years as an abstract idea. Some states in New England threatened to secede over an issue early in the country's history. Nothing came of the threat, but now, in the South, it was being tried in practice.

Those in favor of secession believed that the United States was composed of sovereign states bound to the Constitution by their own consent. If, at a later date, any state decided that its interests were not served by this association, that state could withdraw its consent, declare itself independent, and no longer be a part of the United States.

This view of the rights of states under the Constitution was held by most Southerners. There were several issues which brought the matter to a test, but whether the concern was slavery or tariffs or loss of political power or something else, it all came down to the same question: could a state, once it decided it had a justifiable cause, vote to actually leave the Union? Of course, there were also those who said that secession was really nothing but rebellion, and they were just as dedicated to preserving the Union, whatever the cost.

With the presidential election of November 1860, secession ceased to be a theory. The Democrats had fragmented so much that the new Republican Party, participating in only its second national election, was able to elect its candidate, Abraham Lincoln. Because of his stand on many things, slavery among them, Lincoln was simply unacceptable to the Southern states. He didn't get a single Southern electoral vote, and when his election was announced, many in the South believed that any hope of existing in a union with the Northern states was lost.

In December 1860, South Carolina seceded. In the first few weeks of 1861, it was joined by Mississippi, Florida, Alabama, and Georgia. A convention was then called for the first week in February in Montgomery, Alabama, to form a union of these states and several others that were expected to follow. Few believed that the new president in Washington or the Congress would allow this withdrawal of the Southern states to go unchallenged. So far, though, it had been a war of words, but how long would it last, and what would happen next, nobody knew.

The first three months of 1861 were a time of soul searching and choosing sides for many, both North and South. Whether one was an Army officer faced with the decision of which country to serve, or, like the subjects of this story, just a common husband and wife faced with possible citizenship in a new nation and all that entailed, a person had the feeling that his life was about to change profoundly and forever.

In the next four years, these people would see the Western Hemisphere's greatest conflict. There would be more American blood shed, more American property destroyed, and more American lives uprooted, than at any time in our history—before or since. As 1861 began, no one knew this—not Abraham Lincoln or Jefferson Davis or any of their generals, and certainly not a farmer and part-time schoolteacher and his wife in Maury County, Tennessee, but they would

3

all see it happen in their own way. Volumes have been written by and about the great men mentioned above and many others, as well. No other event in American History has received so much historical and literary attention, but no other event has played so large a part in making our country what it is today.

## CHAPTER TWO

# The Farmer and the President

*February 10, 1861*

For the Warfield family of Hampshire, Tennessee, this day was special. Three years before, Burton Warfield and Nancy Ann Worley had stood before R. B. Trimble, minister of the Gospel, and become man and wife. Burton was then three months short of his twenty-ninth birthday, and Nancy Ann, called Anna, was not quite nineteen.

Burton was already a respected man in the community. He was a farmer, but then almost everybody was, to some degree or other. He was also qualified to teach school in the county, and he and Anna did private tutoring, as well. He was active in the Church of Christ at Cathey's Creek and was a justice of the peace. If the 1860 census figures as to the value of land and personal property owned were any indication, Burton was a prosperous young man.

Anna came from a well-known local family and may have had her eye on Burton (or perhaps the other way around) for a long time. They went to the same church, and she had known him almost all her life because Burton was, in fact, Anna's uncle by marriage. Anna's mother, Elizabeth, had died in 1843, when Anna was four years old. Her older sister, Mary, was seven, and her brother Samuel was two, so her father, Stephen Worley, became a widower with three young children at home. The next year, Stephen married a young widow named Sopronia Warf-

5

ield Dickey, Burton's older sister, who then became Anna's stepmother. Fourteen years later, when Burton and Anna married, Stephen Worley, who was already Burton's brother-in-law, became his father-in-law as well.

In the three years they had been married, there had been some sad times, but for the most part, life had been good. Unfortunately, Burton's father, Mathais, died three months after the wedding. He had come to Columbia, Tennessee, in 1811, and was one of the first cabinetmakers to set up shop. Burton and Anna took his widowed mother in to live with them, and Burton acted as executor and settled his father's estate. The next year, a son was born, and they named him Kaeiser, after Burton's mother's family.

This third anniversary came at a time of great uncertainty. The Warfields were not so far out in the backwoods that they didn't know what was happening. They knew their world was changing; they just couldn't see the shape of the new one yet. On this same day, about 350 miles southwest as the crow flies, an older couple was about to get a much clearer look at their own future.

A few weeks before, Senator Jefferson Davis of Mississippi, having received official word that his state had seceded from the union, made his farewell speech on the floor of the United States Senate and like so many other Southerners, went home to offer his services to his own state. Davis was convinced that war was coming, and as a graduate of West Point and a former Secretary of War under Franklin Pierce, he felt his best service would be as a soldier. Governor J. J. Pettus agreed and immediately appointed Davis to lead the Mississippi Volunteers with the rank of major general, which was exactly what Davis had requested. While they waited for the governor to call up the state's troops, Davis and his wife Varina went home to their plantation on the Mississippi River, about twenty miles below Vicksburg.

On February 10, 1861, as the Warfields celebrated their anniversary in Tennessee, Jeff and Varina Davis walked in their garden at Brierfield Plantation, enjoying the early spring weather and pruning a rose bush. Just then, a messenger brought a telegram. Mrs. Davis would later remember that her husband read it like a man seeing his death sentence. It was from the convention being held in Montgomery, Alabama, and it said:

*Sir:*

*We are directed to inform you that you are this day unanimously elected President of the Provisional Government of the Confederate States of America, and to request you to come to Montgomery immediately. We send also a special messenger. Do not wait for him.*

*R. Toombs, R. Barnwell Rhett*

Jefferson Davis was not to be a soldier, after all. He left the next day for Montgomery. His train stopped many times along the way, and he told the cheering crowds the same thing he had told Governor Pettus when he came home from Washington—prepare for a long and bloody war—but neither the governor nor the cheering crowds believed him.[1]

---

1 Shelby Foote, *The Civil War, A Narrative* (New York: Random House, 1958), 16-17.

*Stephen Worley*
*Anna (Worley) Warfield's father and Burton Warfield's father in law.*
*Since his second marriage was to one of Burton's older sisters,*
*he was Burton's brother in law as well.*
*Courtesy of Loreace Concannon. Copy by Gary Concannon and Ted Sahd*

## CHAPTER THREE
## *Gone for Soldiers*

Even with the formation of the Confederate States and Jefferson Davis' election as its president, Tennessee's inclusion in the Confederacy was far from a sure thing. There was a lot of Union sympathy, especially in East Tennessee. In Maury County, where the Warfields lived, there were mixed feelings. Like most Southerners, the citizens believed in a state's right to secede and were not about to condemn their neighbor states for doing so. On the other hand, they had a long history of commitment to the Union. While the course of events in Washington angered many, especially in the western part of the state, Tennessee was not as much a hotbed of discontent as South Carolina or other places. Maury County even had a past president of its own—James K. Polk.

Leaving the Union would be a great emotional leap for many Tennesseans. Feelings were so divided in the state that the resolution to leave the Union was defeated when it was first proposed on February 9, 1861. When Southern troops under General Beauregard fired on the U. S. garrison at Fort Sumter in Charleston harbor on April 12, however, everything changed.

All over the South, units began organizing. By early May, even though Tennessee had not yet formally withdrawn from the Union, Governor Harris began to call for volunteers to provide for the defense of the state.

On May 12, a group of eighty men from western Maury County, near the town of Hampshire organized a cavalry company. Most of these men farmed the land around the town, and were therefore able to meet the first and most basic requirement of a cavalryman—they each had a horse. One of these men was Burton Warfield. Throughout the war, a Confederate cavalryman's horse was his personal property, not the state's, and its value was assessed and recorded. On Burton's enlistment papers, his horse is valued at $125.[2]

As the recruits assembled, old soldiers came forward to drill and train the new ones. A certain Colonel Bowen put the new company through its paces for the rest of May until it was called to Columbia to be properly sworn in. Maj. S. L. Scudder did the honors on June 5, 1861. The term of enlistment was twelve months. Three days later, Tennessee passed a second resolution of secession by a two-thirds majority.

The men may have been excited by the prospect of being dashing Southern cavalrymen, but it is doubtful that many of their wives and sweethearts saw it that way. Anna could not have enjoyed the prospect of Burton going off to war just then. Twenty-two years old, she was seven months pregnant with their second child.

Burton's company moved south to Camp Lee near Mt. Pleasant, Tennessee, and was combined with four other companies to form the Second Battalion, Tennessee Cavalry. Toward the end of July, the battalion was ordered to march north to Camp Trousdale near the Kentucky line. This being the first march the battalion had ever made, there was a lot to learn. One soldier later wrote: "I am inclined to think that when we left Mt. Pleasant we had more cooking vessels, camping supplies,

---

2 Tennessee State Archives, Nashville, Tennessee. Civil War records of Burton Warfield, hereafter referred to as Warfield Official Records. JRK

tents, wagons etc. to move than Joseph E. Johnson's entire army had when it surrendered near Charlotte, N.C." He also said that his company commander, Capt. Andrew Polk, made the trip in a fine carriage with a driver and extra horses.[3]

At Camp Trousdale, the Second Battalion was attached to the Third Tennessee Infantry, commanded by Col. John C. Brown, and on August 12, they were formally transferred from state service to the Army of the Confederate States of America. By the middle of September, they were moving across the line into Kentucky as the advance party of a division under Gen. Simon Buckner. All this was set in motion by one man.[4]

3 Capt. W. T. Hardison, *Confederate Veteran*, Vol. 27, No. 11, (November, 1919), 430.
4 John Barrien Lindsley, *Military Annals of Tennessee* (Nashville: J. M. Lindsley & Co., 1886), 2:883.

CHAPTER FOUR
## *Confederate Forces–Unified Command*

When it became clear that war would certainly come, there began a scramble for military talent, both in the U. S. Army and Navy and in their newborn counterparts in the Confederacy, and existing military professionals went where their conscience led them. The old peacetime military was tiny compared to the numbers which would be required before this conflict was over, so the available pool of experienced leadership—especially men who had actually commanded large numbers of troops in the field—was vanishingly small.

The officer corps of the old Regular Army was rather like a small, exclusive club where most of the ranking officers knew each other personally. They were almost all West Point graduates, and many had previously served together. As a junior officer, James Longstreet of Georgia had stood as a groomsman at the wedding of his friend and fellow officer Ulysses S. "Sam" Grant of Illinois to Julia Dent. At Gettysburg, Confederate Gen. Lewis Armistead would be mortally wounded leading a part of "Picket's Charge" against a Union position held by his best friend in the pre-war army, Union Gen. Winfield Scott Hancock, who was also seriously wounded a few yards away at about the same time. As he was dying, Armistead requested that his personal Bible be given to Gen. Hancock's wife. This war would be very personal.

As in all such competitions for scarce resources, there would be some prizes better than others. In this case, most people—on both sides—agreed on the number one pick, and there was really never any question but that Jeff Davis and the South would get him. Davis is quoted as saying, "I hoped and expected that I had others that would prove generals, but I knew I had one, and that was Sidney Johnston." He called him "the greatest soldier, the ablest man, civil or military, Confederate or Federal, then living."[5]

Albert Sidney Johnston of Kentucky was two years ahead of Jefferson Davis at West Point and was probably the most experienced officer active in the U. S. Army in the critical area of actually commanding troops in the field. When the war came, Johnston was fifty-eight years old and commanding the Department of the Pacific, headquartered in San Francisco. He resigned from the U. S. Army and led a small group of officers three thousand miles, by land and sea, to Richmond. It was all this, and perhaps a little left-over hero worship on President Davis' part, that gained him the position of the most senior Confederate general in the field, second only to the Adjutant General of the nation, ranking even the almost equally famous Robert E. Lee, who had been offered command of the Union Army before declining in favor of his native state of Virginia.[6]

If Jeff Davis had an ace in his hand, this man was it, and he knew exactly where he had to play him. Albert Sidney Johnston was commissioned a full general and given command of a huge area known as "The West." His job was to hold a line beginning at about the Cumberland Gap in eastern Kentucky, west to the Mississippi River, across southern Missouri, on into the Indian Territory and Texas and into the desert

---

5 Foote, *The Civil War*, 169.
6 Ibid., 25.

beyond. Even on paper, such an assignment would take one's breath away. In actual practice, it would prove impossible.

When General Johnston arrived in Nashville in the middle of September 1861, one of the first people to meet him was Simon Buckner, an experienced officer and former head of the Kentucky Guard. He immediately offered his services and was given a brigadier's commission. His first assignment was to take the troops around Camp Trousdale and move north to secure Bowling Green, Kentucky. This was the force that included Burton Warfield's Second Battalion, Tennessee Cavalry and initially numbered about four thousand men.[7]

By the middle of October 1861, Burton Warfield had been a soldier for about four and a half months. He was beginning to realize that most of a soldier's life consisted of everything else but fighting. More to the point, he had been primarily in camp for the last month, with occasional "scouts," or small unit reconnaissance missions, to break the boredom. He was also finding out that camp life with a Civil War army could be every bit as deadly as enemy bullets. It is at this point that we have Burton's first surviving letter home.

It is obvious that Burton wasn't having a good time. He was in the hospital. He was lonely. He was homesick. All his buddies had gone on an assignment. It was just he and one other friend left behind, sick. Some of his clothes were worn out. He wanted to see his wife. He just wanted to go home.

—∿—

---

7 Ibid., 170.

Bowling green

Oct 14 1861

Dear Anna

*I am now at the hospital and not much prospect of getting home. I received 2 letters from you night before last by Billy Wilkes which were verry[8] welcome messengers to me indeed. I was verry glad to know that you were all well. I feel like I was well if I only could gain my strenth. I am verry weak and have a very bad cough. I am sorry you have been so distressed by the false stories with regard to my being captured by the enemy. It is true I have been in some perilous places in passing through an enemy county where they were lying in ambush on all sides. I helped take several of them prisoners but they did not disturb me. I was taken sick and did not go the whole scout. Our battalion are all gone to Green River or some where in that section. There is none of our company here but Jim Sargent and myself. Jim has the measels. He brought the letter to me you spoke of. He was here but a day or two before he took the measels. There are 50 or 60 thousand troops here now. They are going on still north of this. There is a great battle expected in a short time up about Louisville.[9] I do want to see you so bad, can't you come up here and stay a few days? You will be*

---

8  As much as possible, I have left the text as Burton or Anna wrote it. One example is the word "verry." It is not a typo. Burton consistently spelled it with the extra "R," while Anna did not. JRK

9  Foote, *The Civil War*, 175. These comments by Burton indicate the success of General Johnston's efforts to mislead the Union commanders as to his true strength and intentions. In order to buy some time and play on the natural tendency of the opposing commanders to overestimate their opposition, Johnston purposely led his own press to believe that he had a much larger force, and was seriously considering an offensive move toward the Ohio River at Louisville or even Cincinnati. He fooled not only Burton, a lowly cavalryman, but the Union commanders, as well. Johnston's actual troop strength around Bowling Green was never above about 25,000. The movement of Burton's Battalion "to Green River" probably refers to the area around Munfordsville, Kentucky, where they had several brief fights with small Union units.

taken care of here. There are some ladies here from Tenn staying at the hospital. If you could get some person to come with you you could get here directly. It would not cost you much, and maybe I would get to go home with you. You could talk to the doctor here and have more influence over him than anyone else. I am going to stay here until I get able for duty if they don't send me home if it is till Christmas. I rcvd a pair of suspenders yesterday you sent me. They were brought to the hospital. I do not know who brought them. Billy Wilkes perhaps. He did not say anything about them the night before. He probably forgot them and sent them to me the next morning. As regards my clothes, you had better send them or bring them yourself. I would much rather see you than the clothes. I wrote you last week by Jerry Hobson. If you should come here inquire for the general hospital. It is close to the depot. I have been here but a few days. I staid in camp as long as the boys remained here. I have nothing more of interest to write. As I can't come I ask you to come. Give my love to all

As ever yours Burton

—⁕—

The next letter came only five days later and was a report on Burton's continuing but still unsuccessful effort to get a furlough home because of illness.

—⁕—

*Boling green*
*Oct 19th 1861*
*Dear Anna*

I came in 2 hours yesterday of getting a furlow home. Gen. Johnson told the Dr. of the Hospital to furlow the sick home and he wrote my furlow and before it could be signed by Col. Brown the order was counter-manded so I am here yet. They are furlowing some to the Gen. Hospital at Nashville. I will try and get a furlow to Nashville and probably I can get a furlow from there home. If you come up here you must call at the Hospital at Nashville. You will have to stay there about 1 hour any how before you get a train for Boling green. I do not know what to say about my clothes yet if you have not sent them already. I was called to supper before I finished this letter. I will hardly call this a letter it is so short! My health is not improving much. I must close for the present so goodbye

Burton

—⁓—

## CHAPTER FIVE

# *Union Forces—Divided Command*

*T*he Union forces facing General Johnston east of the Mississippi River outnumbered him almost two to one—a fact he went to great lengths to conceal—but they had their own problems which worked to his advantage. When Johnston arrived in Nashville in mid-September, he had command of all Confederate troops holding the line in southern Kentucky, as well as those across the Mississippi in southern Missouri and northern Arkansas. The Union command structure divided this area into two departments with different, and often competing, commanders. Also, while General Johnston remained in command until his death the following April, the Union side changed commanders during that time. This confusion in the Northern command structure was not enough to offset the presence of forty thousand additional troops, but it did give Johnston more time to prepare than he would have had otherwise. In the end, though, the result would be the same.

In September 1861, Johnston had two opposite numbers on the Union side. John Charles Fremont commanded the Department of the West with his headquarters in Saint Louis. Kentucky fell under the command of the hero of Ft. Sumter, Robert Anderson. Fremont, the explorer of the far West and friend of Kit Carson, had plenty to occupy him in Missouri. His forces had been defeated at Wilson Creek the month before, and now he had Confederate troops under Gen. Sterling Price wandering free in the western part of the state. Fremont had also made some civil policies of his own without Lincoln's approval and was seen in Washington as a "loose cannon." General Anderson was a different matter. He was the hero of Fort Sumter and a very capable soldier, but not in the best of health. He was, in fact, remaining on active duty against the advice of his doctor.

This, then, was the situation at the time Burton wrote his first two letters. Kentucky was officially trying to remain neutral and keep out both Union and Confederate forces, but there was little hope of that. Before long, Confederates under Leonidas Polk moved up to Columbus, Kentucky, and Union forces under Grant moved into Paducah. By the time Burton and his unit moved into Bowling Green, both sides were fighting over the supposedly neutral state.

Just at the time Burton was writing, however, the Union commanders were changing. The first to go was Anderson. His doctors had been right. By the middle of October, he had gone on sick leave and been replaced by William T. Sherman.[10] Fremont lasted a couple of weeks longer by refusing to see anyone who might be bringing the official orders relieving him, but by the first of November, he was gone also.

The big change, however, came in Washington. On November 1, 1861, Gen. George McClellan replaced Winfield Scott as the commander of all Union armies and immediately reorganized the departments in the West. He sent Gen. Henry Halleck to Saint Louis and expanded his department eastward to include all of Kentucky west of the Cumberland River. To command the remainder of Kentucky, he picked Gen. Don

---

10 Ibid., 88.

Carlos Buell to replace Sherman. Due to the false information Johnston had been feeding the press, Sherman believed himself vastly outnumbered and daily expected the Confederates to launch an offensive his way. Since he had taken command in Cincinnati, Sherman's messages to the War Department had become more and more alarmist.

After Buell took command, Sherman was sent to Saint Louis where Halleck eventually put him on a leave of absence and called his wife to take him home to recover his composure. McClellan's comment was more to the point, if less diplomatic. "Sherman's gone in the head," he said.[11] These two senior commanders—Halleck and Buell—were the opposition General Johnston faced from November 1861, until the battle of Shiloh the following April.

Of course, Confederate cavalryman Burton Warfield didn't move in the same circles as the generals just mentioned. During this time he was more involved in recovering his health and in the operations of his company. He got over the illness he mentioned in his first letters and participated in almost all the missions of the Second Battalion through the end of the year. These missions, or "scouts," sometimes resulted in short firefights or the capture of a few prisoners, but more often they meant enduring hard riding, short rations, and bad weather in order to keep tabs on the enemy.

Burton's next letter was written two days before Christmas. Knowing he couldn't be home for the holiday, he dealt with personal and family matters, including warning Anna that she must address his letters correctly because he thought some of them were going to another Warfield in a nearby unit. It must have been hard to sit in camp and write this letter instead of being home with his wife and two children.

---

11 Ibid., 148.

The youngest was little Mary Burton "Minnie" Warfield, just four months old, whom Burton had never seen.

—⁂—

*Camp Covington near Bowling green*

*Dec. 23, 1861*

*Dear Anna,*

*I avail myself of another oportunity of writing you a few lines. I sent you 2 letters, one by Leutinant Brooks, the other by Jerry Hobson and verry probable you will get this one before either of the others. We are still here not moved yet, but how soon we may I can't tell. Twelve thousand troops left here this morning for Green river. It is quite cold here now some snow on the ground just enough to make it cold. I need an overcoat verry much. I can't get one here without paying four prices for it. The letters you send me by mail are taken out I expect by the Warfield in the Arkansas regiment, unless you direct them to 2nd Battalion Tenn. Cavalry. You must be your own judge about selling more pork to Bro Young than I engaged. It is worth more than what I sold at. Lonny found his gloves the other day. They were rolled up in a pair of drawers. He had not undone them before.[12] I staid with Gray White night before last and sat up all night. He is some better now. He may get well by good attention. I detail a nurse for him every day. If you wish to send me anything, Jerry Hobson will bring it if your Pa does not come. He is going to bring a great many things for the boys such as butter, sausage meat etc. He will be up some time after Christmas. I will need another pr of socks or 2. The pair I put on when I started had holes in them in less than two weeks. If I had the yarn and a needle I could darn them myself. I am well. Give my regards to all. Write soon.*

---

12 "Lonny" is Anna's younger brother, Samuel Alonzo Worley. He was twenty years old and a private in Burton's unit and will be mentioned several more times.

Goodbye

Burton

—〰—

Just after New Year's Day, 1862, Burton wrote his next letter. He was still homesick, but he included a passage to show that what he had seen in Kentucky had changed him and hardened his resolve to protect his own state. There was also the beginning of the feeling that something was going to happen to break the stalemate of the past months.

—〰—

*Jan 5* [1862][13]

*Dear Anna*

*You can't imagine how much I think of you and desire to be at home to enjoy the peace and quietude of the family circle. Yet when I see the desolation of the fertil fields and fine estates of the people of Kentucky, and to see the women and gray headed sires fleeing from the oppression and insults of the invaders of these once happy homes is enough to excite the patriotism of every brave son of Tennessee to keep the same scenes of deso-lation and destruction from being enacted upon their own soil and their own homes. We should bear the hardships and inconveniences of camp life with out a murmur while we know that our friends at home, and those we hold most dear, are secure from the desolating tread of an army much like that of an invading foe. This is a day of leisure with me. I have written to you to day, and this evening I was again in the Col & [?] and finding plenty of paper and ink, I could not resist the feeling of writing you a few more lines. The scouting party has not got in yet. There is some prospect of a fight to day. It is quite probable they will have a skirmish. We will hear*

---

13 This letter is only dated "Jan 5," but from internal evidence, the year must have been 1862. JRK

tonight or in the morning if anything of importance occurs. I will inform you before I start this letter. Since I wrote the other letter to day some person brought a package of letters from Bowling green. I was so much ...
[page torn]

Good bye

Burton

[on back of above]

*Jan. 6th*

The boys returned last night from the scout. Nothing of importance occurred. The weather quite cold and unpleasant this morning. I don't feel so well this morning. BW

—∾—

While Burton and his unit and the rest of the Confederate troops around Bowling Green waited and watched and tried to make their camps a little more comfortable in the worsening winter weather, events that would break the stalemate were finally in motion on the Union side.

CHAPTER SIX
# Union Forces—War and Politics

Almost from the time he took command of the Department of the West, Henry Halleck wanted to consolidate his command and that of Buell in eastern Kentucky and form one department as the Confederates had done—as long as he was chosen as its commander, of course. General Buell had much the same thing in mind, and both men knew it. The final decision, however, was up to General McClellan in Washington. Because of this, neither Buell nor Halleck was anxious to cooperate in a strategy that might give an advantage to the other in the game of War Department politics. Besides, both commanders had their own problems.

Halleck arrived at Saint Louis in early November 1861 to find a department which his predecessor had left in chaos. Since then, he had spent his time trying to bring some order to his command, and didn't feel ready for offensive action yet. In Buell's case, he was feeling pressure from the White House itself.

President Lincoln was concerned about the many Union sympathizers in east Tennessee. There were stories of persecution and even hangings by the Confederate authorities, and Lincoln was pressing his military commanders to make a move toward Knoxville. Headquartered in Cincinnati, Buell's command was the obvious force to use, but he protested that the country between him and Knoxville was very poor and he would be unable to supply his army during such an advance. Buell preferred to work his way along the railroad toward Bowling Green and then on south to Nashville, but Washington kept insisting on a move to the southeast.

General Johnston knew that the confusion and infighting in the Northern ranks would not last forever. He spent the time from September until early January doing his best with what he could pull together. He sent several appeals to President Davis for more of everything—men, arms, and supplies—and kept his real situation secret from all but a few of his staff. By early January, he had a little over 50,000 men east of the Mississippi River to face about 90,000 on the Union side. Most of these Confederate troops were divided to cover four key positions.

Gen. Leonidas Polk covered the Mississippi River with 17,000 men from his position at Columbus, Kentucky. Polk's opposite number, a few miles north at Cairo, Illinois, was a little known Union brigadier named Ulysses S. Grant with 20,000 troops.

William Hardee commanded the area around Bowling Green, Kentucky, but instead of the fifty to 60 sixty thousand troops Burton talks about in his letters, he actually had only 25,000 to face Buell's army of 60,000.

In the east, guarding the Cumberland Gap and standing in the way of the move toward Knoxville, which Lincoln continued to demand, Gen. George Crittenden had barely 4,000 men whose field commander was a newspaper editor with no military experience, but excellent political connections, and the singular name of Felix K. Zollicoffer. He faced Buell's subordinate, George Thomas and about 8,000 Union troops.

Finally, there were about 4,500 assorted soldiers, artillerymen, and engineers under Lloyd Tilghman, who were working frantically to shore up the defenses at the two forts that covered the Tennessee and Cumberland Rivers. It was only a matter of time before this thin line would be tested, and anyone's guess where the test might come.[14] As it happened, the unraveling of the Confederate line began in southeast Kentucky.

---

14 Foote, *The Civil War*, 171-172. Johnston's order of battle, troop strength, and subordinate commanders are available from many other sources, as well.

## Chapter Seven
# *The Professional and the Politician*

Maj. Gen. George Crittenden and Brig. Gen. Felix Zollicoffer were a poor team. Though he was a professional soldier, there had long been talk of Crittenden's drinking problems, and while Zollicoffer was a first rate politician and stump orator, he had no experience in actual military operations. This combination was a disaster looking for a place to happen. The place turned out to be near Mill Springs, Kentucky.

In early January 1862, Zollicoffer had been ordered northwest from the Cumberland Gap to the south bank of the rain-swollen Cumberland River. The newspaperman, however, decided that the better campsites were on the north bank and moved his men across. Despite orders from Crittenden to re-cross the river, Zollicoffer and his men were still on the north side when his commander finally arrived on the scene the second week in January. To add to the Confederates' woes, information began coming in that a superior Union force was on the move toward them. This was Buell's long-resisted move toward East Tennessee, finally put in motion and led by Gen. George Thomas. Gen. Crittenden was now faced with the prospect of a battle in which his untried troops, under an inexperienced subordinate, would be outnumbered almost two to one and have an all but unfordable river at their back. Had he not already been a hard drinker, this would have driven him to it.

Mercifully, about this time it began to rain. Even though it meant that the river behind Crittenden rose even higher, it also forced Thomas to divide his troops on opposite banks of another stream and slowed his advance to a crawl. On the seventeenth, after a week of downpours, the Yankees went into camp nine miles away. Having learned that Thomas had stopped to rest and dry out, and that a swollen creek separated his command, Crittenden changed his plans. He decided that he would try a surprise attack while the enemy was divided. Anything was better than waiting to be pushed into the Cumberland River.

As the rain continued, it was now the Confederates who were trying to move men, animals, and guns through the quagmire that passed for roads. They finally closed with the enemy on the morning of January 19. General Zollicoffer was with his men as they drove in the enemy pickets and began, for the moment, to push the Yankees back. Unfortunately, the creek was not as high as they had hoped, so Thomas was able to move men across and reinforce his position, but it was during the height of the battle that the final disaster befell the Confederates. While leading his troops on horseback, General Zollicoffer, who was wearing a conspicuous white raincoat, became disoriented. He rode up to a regiment of what he thought were Confederate troops and began to shout orders. Union Col. Speed S. Fry, leading the troops, suffered no such confusion and ordered a volley to be fired. General Zollicoffer was knocked from the saddle by several minie balls and died with his head on the roots of an oak tree.[15] All this happened in full view of his troops, and that was the last straw. The retreat soon turned into a rout. Many of the Confederates simply went home, and most of what was left of

---

15 Jack D. Welsh, M.D., *Medical Histories of Confederate Generals* (Kent, OH: The Kent State University Press, 1995), 244

Crittenden's army headed toward Nashville and didn't stop for almost eighty miles.

Thomas, of course, would have liked to pursue and finish the job. If military opposition had been the only consideration, he could literally have either marched down the south bank of the Cumberland River and into downtown Nashville or southeast all the way to Knoxville with hardly a shot being fired. Unfortunately, he had almost eight thousand men to feed, and he soon decided that supplying an army that size in the desolate country before him would be impossible. As the rains continued, he had to put his men on half rations and withdraw.[16]

In the army, news and rumors travel fast. Burton's next letter was written only three days after the disaster at Mill Springs, and though some of the rumors he heard were wrong, it's obvious that the rest of the Confederate forces had gone on alert. Action was beginning to pick up all along the line, and we have Burton's first personal account of a skirmish.

—⁂—

*Camp near Oakland*

*Jan 22nd 1862*

*Dear Anna,*

*As I expected we have orders to be ready at a moments warning to leave here. But where we will go I can't tell. The Yankies are making a mighty effort to get to Tennessee. I understand that they have taken Fort Henry on the Tennessee River.[17] We may go 40 or 50 miles above here*

---

16 Foote, *The Civil War*, 176-179. This account of the misfortunes of the Confederate army under Generals Crittenden and Zollicoffer at Mill Springs was condensed from Shelby Foote's much better version.

17 This is evidently a false rumor Burton had heard. While there had been some scouting in the area of Fort Henry, Federal troops would not be seen near there in force for another ten days or so.

to Burksville,[18] but we do not know yet where we will go. We had just got fixed here to live a little comfortable. Some of us have chimnies to our tents. But tomorrow perhaps we will have to strike tents and bid adieu to the little comforts we had in anticipation. We went to Brownsville last Sunday on a scout and had the pleasure of seeing a few Yankees and hear the balls from their minnie muskits whistle over our heads and among our feet. We exchanged a few shots with them but we had the river between us. I shot six times at them. They have longer shooting guns than we have. We were close enough for them to have killed some of us and we them, but they were to cowardly to show themselves long at a time. None were hurt on this side of the river and none that we know of on the other side. After we had ceased and gone near half a mile they came out and shot several volies of musketry at us. The balls whistled and fell all around and among us. I wish if there is any fighting to do in Tennessee they would send us these. I understand that 12 regiments have been ordered from Bowling Green to Tennessee. I don't know whether it is so or not. I will write you again the first opportunity and let you know where we are, but we stay such a short time in a place it is hard for you to keep up with us. You must direct your letters to Bowling Green yet to the case of Capt. Kinzer 2nd Tennessee Cavalry. I can get them from there. Some of the boys have been drawing over coats today from 18 to 21 dollars and I would not give mine for a dozen of them for this service. I have drawn 2 linsey shirts, one plad the other white, and a new pr. boots. I can wear 3 or 4 pair socks in them. I have not time nor nothing more of interest to write. Give my kindest

---

18 This information may have been more reliable since Burksville is on the north side of the Cumberland River and about thirty miles west of Mill Springs. At this time, Thomas would have still been in the area. From Burton's next letter, it seems that the movement was considered, but never actually made.

*regards to all. While I remain yours as ever*
   *Goodbye*
   *Burton*


*P. S. I forgot to tell you that I am well and weigh more than I ever weighed in my life, and flesher than you ever saw me. I am in hopes my health will continue to be good while I am in the service. Has any person ever called on you for my taxes yet. If they do and you have the money you can pay it out that way. Mr. King is at home now if you see him you can tell him about it and he will attend to it for you if he is able to go about any.*
   *(Goodnight) Burton*

—⁂—

While the defeat of the Confederate forces at Mill Springs meant that Johnston's right flank was exposed, Thomas' withdrawal in the face of the weather and the Kentucky wilderness meant that there was no immediate threat from that quarter. Instead of a major realignment of troops, there came a period of uneasy waiting. The first blow had been struck, but it had not been decisive. All the common soldier could do was to try and find a little protection from the bitter winter weather and wait. It was during this period that Burton wrote his next letter.

—⁂—

*Camp Oakland*
*Feb 1st 1862*
*Dear Anna,*

   *If you get so many letters from me that they become troublesome to take care of you can pile them and make a burnt offering. There is another big scout on hand today and but few of us in camp. I feel lonesome. I would have been on the scout myself but it is a detailed scout. I had the detaling to do and other business in camp. If it had been a volunteer scout I would* have been in. It is the 2nd scout only that I have not been in since I have been here. It is a verry disagreeable day, snowing now, rained last night. It is verry mudy, cold, and disagreeable weather. I fear it will produce a great deal of sickness in camp. I was in hopes that Feb. would be more pleasant and agreeable than the month we have just passed through. I hope though the 10th of this month will not be quite as cold as its aniversary of a certain ocasion was. Yet I can't expect it to be as pleasant to me. But let me be where I may whether pressed by the northern blast or faned by a southern breese I will bring to my memory the pleasures of former times.[19] We can get a furlow for sixty days and $50 dollars bounty now if we will come back and enlist for two years or during the war. In fact it is an enlistment itself if we take the furlow home and the bounty money. But I have no notion of biting at that bait. Some of the Battalion will take it how many yet I do not know. I had rather serve my time here until our twelve months is out and risk the chances of going again. When I go again I want to know how and with whom I am going. I will try and get a chance to go home and get Bob before many weeks.[20] We are using rye in our coffee now. Rye will be worth something now if it has to be used in the army as coffee. I expect you will be troubled about getting your molasses and sugar if you have not got them yet. There are so many troops and army store being transported now that you can't get anything else transported. And so many molases are used in the army that they will hardly get any cheper. I want you to send me a pair of socks the first oportunity you have. Esq. Cain Kirk is coming up here sometime before long. It is turning very cold.

Feb 2nd The scout got in last night after midnight. They suffered a

---

19 February 10 would have been Burton and Anna's fourth wedding anniversary.

20 "Bob" is Burton's other horse. He will say more about his horse situation in his next letter.

*good deal with cold. They brought in five prisoners and some other things they took from the Lincolnites. It is freezing cold this morning. It is verry disagreeable writing this morning. Five or six of us in one tent writing at the same time. Perhaps some of my kin folks think I treat them badly by not writing to them. If they do I have the same right to think badly of them. They have a better chance to write to me than I have to them. I would answer any letter written to me if I had a chance and would be glad to do so. I will write to you every chance I get whether I write to anyone else or not. I must quit writing now, the bugle has sounded for church. I don't think I will go today. There is a good deal of excitement among the boys at this moment. The prisners have just been brought out to be carried up to Breckenridge head quarters.[21] A Yankey is a great curiosity to some of the boys. They are bad looking fellows generally. You must write every chance you get. You can get some paper and envelope in Columbia I reckon. I am well. My hair has been coming out ever since I came back. Tell Kaeiser I have got his little deer yet. Have to keep it here to kill old Lincolns. Give my love to all and accept the same yourself*

> *Goodbye*
> *Burton*

—✻—

While Burton and his fellow troopers endured the cold and the boredom and the anxiety in their camps around Bowling Green, things were coming alive at Union General Halleck's headquarters in Saint Louis. Halleck was recovering from the measles when the word of the fight at Mill Springs came in. A victory like that could give Buell a big boost, and unless Halleck could quickly produce a victory of his own,

---

21 This would have been the headquarters of the brigade commanded by John C. Breckinridge, a Kentuckian and vice president under Buchanan.

he might lose out in the race for command of a united Department of the West. Fortunately, Halleck had two things going for him. First, he had a subordinate who was already prepared to go into action at once, and second, he had a not-so-secret weapon. Besides outnumbering the Confederates in soldiers, Halleck had something that was almost totally unmatched by Johnston's forces in Tennessee. He had a "brown water navy."

## CHAPTER EIGHT

## *Two Rivers*

I t doesn't take a military genius to look at a map and realize that, to a great extent, control of Tennessee meant control of its rivers. The Mississippi, on the western border, was critical, of course, but losing control of the Tennessee and Cumberland Rivers would be a disaster. It would cut the state in two and allow the Union forces a free ride from the Ohio River to downtown Nashville to the east, and as far south as northern Alabama. Naturally, General Johnston made their defense a top priority.

Widely separated through most of their courses, the two rivers converge at the Tennessee\Kentucky line. From there until they empty into the Ohio at Paducah, Kentucky, they run parallel just a few miles apart. The danger the rivers posed to the defense of the state was obvious. Even before General Johnston had arrived to take command, work had been started on two forts on the Tennessee side of the line. Fort Henry was on the east bank of the Tennessee, and Fort Donelson was on the west bank of the Cumberland. General Johnston counted himself fortunate, therefore, when Brig. Gen. Lloyd Tilghman reported to him for duty in November. Tilghman was a West Pointer and a civil engineer, and Johnston sent him to oversee the construction of the two forts.

Tilghman was less than pleased with what he found. Fort Donelson needed lots of work, to be sure, but Fort Henry was far worse. Both places needed more of everything—especially cannons—but Fort Henry had other problems, as well. Across the river was high ground that could command the fort if captured by the enemy. As bad as that was, the fort itself was built on such low ground that, after a rainy January, there was some question as to whether Fort Henry's cannons would be submerged by the river before the Yankees even got there. Commenting on the faulty placement of the fort by those who had come before him, Tilghman sadly noted that "The history of military engineering records no parallel to this case."[22] Perhaps, given enough time, something could have been salvaged at Fort Henry, but by early February, time had run out.

Just at the time Halleck received word of Buell's success in eastern Kentucky, General Grant was visiting headquarters to ask that he be allowed to move forward from his base at Cairo, Illinois. Halleck had, for some weeks, had his eye on Fort Henry, but was not ready to move yet, so Grant went back to Cairo disappointed, only to find a bit of good news. Some of his troops under Gen. C. F. Smith had explored up the Tennessee River far enough to actually get a look at Fort Henry. When told of its condition, Grant again requested permission to advance. Halleck, meanwhile, had realized that a move up the Tennessee River might be a chance to regain the upper hand in his competition with Buell, so this time Grant got his permission. By February 3, Grant had almost 17,000 men loaded on steamers, escorted by gunboats—his "brown water navy"—and was on his way up the Tennessee River.[23]

Two days later, the Yankees began landing three miles north of Fort Henry, and General Tilghman knew his situation was hopeless. He

22 Foote, *The Civil War*, 180.
23 Ibid., 181-182.

was outnumbered almost 5 to 1. The 3,000 or so men he did have were only armed with whatever shotgun or squirrel rifle they had brought from home, and finally, thanks to the rising river, only nine of his guns that could fire toward the enemy were still above water. The fate of Fort Henry being obvious, Tilghman decided to save what he could. He and a company of Tennessee artillerymen would stay to man such guns as were still on dry ground, and the infantry and cavalry units would be sent overland to Fort Donelson, twelve miles away.

On the morning of February 6, Grant sent everybody forward in what was supposed to be a combined assault, but it turned out to be an all-Navy show. Seven gunboats, commanded by Commodore Andrew H. Foote, steamed up the river and engaged in a short but intense artillery duel with the fort and its fifty-six defenders. After two hours, with only four guns still in commission and the river lapping at the powder magazine, Tilghman, like a captain going down with his ship, struck his colors. He had done his best. Fort Henry had fallen to the Navy, while Grant's troops were still wading through the marshy countryside. The Army hadn't fired a shot.[24]

With Fort Henry in hand, Grant was confident he could finish the job in short order. He wired General Halleck that "Fort Henry is ours ... I shall take and destroy Fort Donaldson [sic] on the eighth and return to Fort Henry."[25] As it turned out, Grant was a little too optimistic. Fort Donelson would be a far different story.

The false rumor about the fall of Fort Henry that Burton had reported in his letter of January 22 had now come true. By the next

---

24 Ibid., 182-190.
25 Geoffrey Perret, *Ulysses S. Grant, Soldier and President* (New York: Random House, 1997), 164.

day, February 7, the news had spread through the Confederate troops. Perhaps the lull in the action around Bowling Green had given Burton more time off, because it was at this point that he wrote his longest letter of the entire war. He discussed many things, including a somewhat humorous meeting he and others had with General Breckinridge in an attempt to get a furlough. It seemed that the general, being a politician, was able to say "No" in the nicest possible way.

More than anything else, though, the letter revolved around Burton's horse situation. Being a cavalryman, his horse's condition was extremely important. A good mount could be the difference between life and death. Burton was riding a fine mare, which he valued highly, but the months of hard service might have taken a toll on her. He wanted to get her home and take the other horse, Bob, instead, but since he couldn't take her himself, he discussed other ways to do it. He certainly didn't want to be forced into trading the mare away. What Burton didn't know was that his days in Kentucky were almost over. He would be back in Maury County soon, but not the way he expected.

*Note:*

*In 1969, Historic Maury, the journal of the Maury County [Tennessee] Historical Society, published some of the Warfield letters. Most of them simply duplicated the originals still held by the Warfields' great-grandson, which are my primary sources, but a few were new to me. In the case of the February 8 letter, it seems that the original once had an additional page.*

—⁂—

*Camp Oakland*
*Feb 8th 1862*
*Dear Anna,*

*I am sorry to inform you that it is impossible for me to come home* now. I had calculated with some probility of getting home on the plea of taking my mare home to get another horse. But that thing has been tried [in]effectually. Tite Edwards has a mare in the same fix of mine and he could not get to go home although he has not been home since the 17th of August last. Yet we are compelled to get a horse some how. So we have come to the conclusion to get some person down there to bring our horses to us and take our mares back. Do you think we could get Joe Jaggers to bring them up to us. If he will we will pay him well for the trouble enough to satisfy him. Anna we have had, as you are aware, a hard time since we have been in Kentucky, but I fear it is nothing to what we will have to undergo yet. The enemy is closing in on all sides. We heard yesterday of another disaster to our army at Fort Henry. How true it is I cannot say yet I fear it is too true. We will have heavy work here from this time on I have no doubt, and a bloody fight somewhere in this region is inevitable. Yet we may be ordered somewhere else soon. It seems that the enemy is determined to get to Tennessee. But if every soldier we have will do his duty they can never get there to do us much harm. Yet many a brave and gallant son of the south may fall in her defense. But conquer us they never can. They may over run us and despoil us of our homes, but from every hill top and from every secluded spot the missils of death will be sent into their ranks from a foe they can never overcome.

[The following passage is present only in the *Historic Maury* copy of this letter.][26]

*My fingers are numb with cold, it is snowing now and turning cold very fast which will account for my bad scribbling. But to the horse question,*

---

26 *Historic Maury*, *Vol.* 5 (Columbia, TN: Maury County Historical Society, 1969), No. 1, 2-8 & No. 2, 27-31. The material which appears only in the historical society journal is noted in the text. JRK

*Tite is here with me he is sadly disappointed in not getting to go home. He calculated strongly on seeing Mollie in a few days. But this morning he is below zero on the question. But this is not coming to the horse question. The mumps are in camp now. I think I am taking them in one jaw. I had them on one side a long time ago. Tite is scared for fear he will take them. They are going tolerable hard with some of the boys. I have had a verry bad cold and cough since I wrote you last. Tite has a mare and horse at home he wants brought up here if he can get them. If you can get Joe to come or someone else. If they can bring both of his, he wants the mare. Go and see Mollie. she knows which ones to send and you can both make arrangements to have them sent to us. I must have Bob if possible. Maybe you can get Mark Martain to bring our horses to us. My mare is a valu-able animal and I would be glad to get her home. I can't swap horses to any advantage and if I wait much longer I will be compelled to get a horse somehow and will, in all probability, have to make a great sacrifice on my mare. You will think that they will need Bob to plow, but they will have to make some other arrangements about plow stock. Have those two mules broke to work some and the filly also. Make them all work some and it will not be so hard on any of them. Have you commenced plowing yet, got the fences all repaired? Make every edge cut for the time is coming when it will be needed. Have you got seed potatoes (irish).*

[At this point, it appears that Burton was interrupted with news.]

*We have just heard from a Mr. Wilks who took a mare home for Tite E. some time ago he is coming up soon and will bring our horses to us. If he calls for my horse let him have him And let Mollie know he will be there after our horses. Tite has sent word to him directly he will probably get it before you get this. But if you don't hear anything of him soon you can proceed according to the foregoing directions. Wilks lives in Columbia or somewhere near there.*

*We had a scout yesterday and tomorrow will have another I reckon as it will be Sunday and the next day will be the 10th. I don't know how I can get [you] some envelops and paper. I am getting impatient about a letter. I take your want of the necessary articles the cause of the delay. Who is going to administer on Bro. Blocker's estate. And how are you all getting along generally. Have you settled the difficulties in the church and how. It still snows. We have been drawing fresh pork for several days. I don't think it is as healthy as beef it don't agree with us as well as beef. We fatten on beef. Gen. Breckenridge treats us verry well although he would not sign for our furlows to go home. He treated us when we went to sign them so politely and gentlemenly and reasoned the case with us that we were perfectly satisfied that we had no business home. If he signed one he would have to sign a hundred of the same sort and probably our service will be needed at any time. We know not at what time we will have to go into a fight or move to some other point.*

*They are calling for me now at the comissary to draw provisions. I will send some of the other boys and finish [this] letter. Did you ever get any corn from Henry Edwards. I must try and get some money to pay some of my debts when I get home. We have not drawn any more money yet. Don't know when we will.*

[The original copy of the letter resumes.]

*Anna I have nothing more of interest to write. I have some things that I expected to tell you in person soon. But being disappointed in that pleasure I will defer it until I get to see you, which will not be longer than four months I hope.*[27] *Yet we may be pressed for 90 days after our time is out. There is some talk of 12 months volunteers being pressed for 2 years longer, but I can't think they will do that. If they want to press anybody*

---

27 This would be the end of his one-year enlistment.

*let them press some of the cowardly scamps that are at home who can retire to their feathered couches protected and made secure by us who are undergoing the rigors of winter and the perils of the soldier while they can, undisturbed in their repose sleep without a dread upon their minds, dream sweetly of home comforts and ponder in their minds in what manner they can swindle the country and the families of the volunteers. I say press them.*[28] *Nothing more at present. Give my kindest regards to all. Kiss the little ones for me and do the best you can for yourself. Write soon.*

> *Yours truly,*

> *Burton*

*P. S.*

*We have just heard from Fort Donelson on Cumberland River the report is that they are fighting there and that Col Gantt's Battalion of Cavalry were cut to pieces but I don't credit the report.*[29] *It may be probable there was a fight there. Good night B*

---

28 Thomas B. Buell, *The Warrior Generals* (New York: Three Rivers Press, 1997), 127. Burton's feelings on the matter of extending the commitments of the twelve-month volunteers are understandable since he has only a little over four months left to serve. So is his opinion of those men who have managed to evade serving. His fears of being "pressed" also turned out to be well founded. Two months after he wrote this letter, the Confederate government passed a draft law in which all able-bodied men from 18 to 35 (later 45) were liable for three years of service. More important for Burton, all men already in uniform were "pressed" for three years also (later for the duration of the war).

29 *Tennesseans in the Civil War, Part 1* (Nashville, TN: Civil War Centennial Commission, 1964), 66. Burton is interested in this unit because many of the men were from Maury County. The unit was the Ninth Battalion Tennessee Cavalry commanded by Lt. Col. George Gantt. It had been raised in November and had seen no active service. It was actually pulled out of a training camp and sent to Fort Henry in mid-January. At the time of Burton's letter, the Ninth had not been "cut to pieces" at all. It had not fired a shot, but had retired to Fort Donelson with the rest of the troops from Fort Henry. At Fort Donelson, however, Lt. Col. Gantt was criticized by Col. N. B. Forrest for failing to fight and for refusing an order to come with Forrest when he broke out of the Union lines on February 15. All but one company of the Ninth were taken prisoner at Fort Donelson on February 16. Lt. Col. Gantt, however, will reappear in Burton's story.

—w—

Burton had no way of knowing as he rambled on about his horse situation, his debts, and his farm concerns, that a decision had already been made to send him back toward home. When Fort Henry fell, General Johnston decided that, in order to save his army from being trapped, he would have to retreat south of the Cumberland River. He reinforced the troops at Fort Donelson, hoping they could hold out long enough to give him the time he needed and then be able to withdraw and join him near Nashville. Johnston and his staff left Bowling Green on February 11 with the rest of the troops around Bowling Green following soon after. Burton spent long hours in the saddle as his unit formed the rear guard of the army.

Meanwhile, as Burton and his friends in the Second Battalion, Tennessee Cavalry and the rest of General Johnston's army in central Kentucky were retreating into Middle Tennessee, General Grant was having troubles of his own. In spite of his optimistic message to his commander after the fall of Fort Henry, it was six days before he set out to capture Fort Donelson. On February 12, the day of the march, the weather was fine and everybody was in good spirits. That night, however, as they reached the area around the fort on the Cumberland River, the spring day gave way to a bitter winter night. The Union troops shivered in the cold and roasted some of the semi-wild pigs that roamed the countryside.[30] Fort Donelson was not going to be a small skirmish between a few Navy gunboats and fifty or so artillerymen like Fort Henry. Grant would eventually put over 27,000 men in the field around the fort against about 17,500 well dug-in Confederates.

---

30 Perret, *Ulysses S. Grant*, 167.

On February 14, Commodore Foote sent his ironclads up the Cumberland to reduce Fort Donelson by naval gunfire. The Confederate guns at Fort Donelson, however, were not placed in a swamp like the ones at Fort Henry, but nicely situated on a bluff overlooking the river. As a result, the Union gunboats were soundly thrashed and forced to withdraw. Fort Henry had been an all-Navy show, but if Fort Donelson was to be taken, it would be up to General Grant and his infantry.

The day after the repulse of the Federal gunboats, a sharp battle commenced as the Confederates tried to break out through Grant's lines, but were unsuccessful. Later that night, the two senior Confederate generals fled up the river, leaving Simon Buckner, a professional soldier and evidently made of sterner stuff, to become the first Confederate general to request surrender terms from his Union counterpart.[31] Grant's reply would become part of his legend: "No terms except unconditional surrender can be accepted. I propose to move immediately on your works."[32] Buckner thought the reply a little harsh, but had no choice but to comply.

Grant and Buckner were old friends and West Point classmates. In 1854, when Grant left the regular army, broke and in semi-disgrace, Buckner loaned him money to get home from California. Now, eight years later with the tables turned, Grant offered to return the favor, but Buckner, ever the Kentucky gentleman, declined.[33]

To the Northern press, in need of heroes, Ulysses S. Grant, victor of Fort Donelson, became "Unconditional Surrender" Grant. Between 12,000 and 15,000 Confederate troops were captured. In a letter to his

---

31 Foote, *The Civil War*, 212.
32 Perret, *Ulysses S. Grant*, 173.
33 Foote, *The Civil War*, 213.

wife, Julia, Grant modestly noted that it was the largest capture of enemy troops ever made in North America up until that time—almost twice the number of British troops captured by Washington at Yorktown.[34] Unknown to the Union generals, who had consistently overestimated Confederate strength, it was also almost one-third of General Johnston's troop strength east of the Mississippi.[35]

Burton Warfield and the Second Battalion, Tennessee Cavalry arrived on the north bank of the Cumberland River opposite Nashville just in time to witness the state capital on the verge of panic. The news of the fall of Fort Donelson arrived just as many of the citizens were attending church services on Sunday morning, February 16, about the same time as the leading elements of Johnston's retreating army appeared across the river. All that day and most of the next, the units crossed the river and continued through the city, heading south to Murfreesboro. Some of the soldiers deserted and mingled with the crowds of looters who began to break into the large military warehouses.[36] Burton's unit, as rear guard, crossed the river on the railroad bridge late on Monday afternoon and followed the main body toward Murfreesboro.[37]

Not only was Nashville the capital of the state, it was also the main supply depot for the Confederate army in Middle Tennessee, containing huge stockpiles of food and munitions. Even so, General Johnston had no plans to defend it, to the great relief of the city fathers who had visions of their city being destroyed by the advancing Union armies. As for the supplies, the task of salvaging as much as possible fell to Lt. Col. Nathan

---

34 Perret, *Ulysses S. Grant*, 174.
35 Larry J. Daniel, *Shiloh* (New York: Simon & Schuster, 1997), 41.
36 Ibid., 41.
37 Lindsley, *Military Annals*, 884.

Bedford Forrest. He had escaped from Fort Donelson with something over five hundred men and entered the city the day after Burton's cavalry company passed through. During the next five days, Forrest restored some semblance of order, often at the point of his sword, commandeered every wagon and railroad car he could find, and moved a large quantity of military stores out of the Union army's reach. Even so, when he left to join Johnston at Murfreesboro on February 23, he left behind over a half-million pounds of pork, ten thousand pairs of shoes, and fifty cannons, all of which were either captured by the enemy or looted by the local citizens.[38]

---

38 Daniel, *Shiloh*, 43.

## CHAPTER NINE
# *Retreat and Regroup*

he day after Forrest and his troopers left the city, Union Gen.
Don Carlos Buell's troops finally arrived on the north bank of
the Cumberland River opposite Nashville, having marched from
Bowling Green, Kentucky. Still believing he was outnumbered by
Johnston's Confederate army,[39] Buell was more than content to occupy
the city and build up his own forces. In fact, Union forces in and
around Nashville on that day, February 24, 1862, almost matched the
Confederate forces. After picking up some scattered units and escapees
from Fort Donelson, General Johnston could muster about 17,000 men,
in and around Murfreesboro.[40] In any case, four days later, Johnston
was on the move again.

On February 28, the Confederate army pulled out of Murfrees-
boro and headed southwest toward Alabama. As usual, the cavalry
went ahead, scouting the roads and watching for the enemy. Burton's
Second Battalion, Tennessee Cavalry, now under the command of
Lt. Col. J. B. Biffle, was part of this effort, covering the area around
Columbia and Maury County, well-known country to all those local

---

39 Ibid., 59. Buell himself believed Johnston's strength at Murfreesboro to be as high as
30,000 troops.
40 Ibid., 44.

boys. Unfortunately, they couldn't stop and visit since the army was moving on toward the Tennessee River.

Burton's little cavalry battalion was only a small cog in a large operation. The army was moving in several columns, and heavy rain made the going slow for all concerned. Burton's unit finally reached Decatur, Alabama, about the twentieth of March.[41] Their job, using Decatur as a base, then became scouting northward back into Tennessee and reporting on Union troops moving south and west from Nashville. The information they and other cavalry units sent back would be crucial to General Johnston as he planned his next move.

It was clear to both General Beauregard, who was bringing forces from West Tennessee and as far away as Mobile, Alabama, and concentrating them at Corinth, Mississippi, and General Johnston, who was trying to reach him with what remained of the forces from Kentucky, that they were engaged in a race. By March 10, Johnston had reached Decatur, with most of his troops still strung out back to the Tennessee line. Two days later, Union transports began arriving at Savannah, Tennessee, only about twenty-five miles, as the crow flies, north of Corinth. Two days after that, a Union gunboat raided as far upriver as the Alabama line. Clearly, the Yankees had come in force. This was Grant's army, now reinforced after its victory at Fort Donelson, which had come south and was moving into camp on the west bank of the Tennessee River at a place called Pittsburg Landing.

General Johnston finally arrived at Corinth on March 22.[42] Even though there were many details still to be discovered about the enemy forces, Johnston, Beauregard, and the rest of the senior Confederate

---

41 Ibid., 90.
42 Ibid.

generals knew the overall picture well enough. Within about fifteen miles of Confederate Headquarters at Corinth, General Grant's Army of the Tennessee, which would eventually number almost 50,000 men, was going into camp. At Nashville, 130 miles to the northeast, was the Union Army of the Ohio under Gen. Don Carlos Buell. In fact, Johnston's scouts, including Burton's cavalry unit, would shortly report that the major part of that army—37,000 men—was already marching to reinforce Grant. On the day Johnston reached Corinth, Buell's lead elements were only eighty miles away, trying to ford the swollen Duck River at Columbia, Tennessee. Against these two Union armies, totaling about 85,000 troops, Johnston could field about 44,000 men.[43] Being so outnumbered, he continued to search for men, even to the point of looking west of the Mississippi.

At the beginning of March, the Confederates had an army of 17,000 men in northwest Arkansas under Gen. Earl Van Dorn. On March 6, they attacked a smaller Union force (about 10,000 men) under Gen. Samuel Curtis at a place near the Missouri border called Elkhorn Tavern, near the town of Pea Ridge. Even though they outnumbered the Yankees, after two days of fighting, the Confederate army began retreating south toward the Arkansas River. The retreat, however, soon turned into a nightmare.

Most of the 15,700 surviving Confederates had to walk over seventy miles over the Boston Mountains in a cold, driving rain, to reach their camps in the Arkansas River valley. The country was so desolate and sparsely populated that one soldier remarked "even the turkey buzzards would not fly over it." Another man from Louisiana wrote, after staggering into Van Buren a week after the battle, cold and starving, that

---

43 Ibid., 112 and 322.

"the retreat was more disastrous than a dozen battles."[44] To make matters worse, as the exhausted and hungry men stumbled into camps along Frog Bayou, near a little settlement which, a few years later, would become Alma, Arkansas, word came from General Johnston, instructing Van Dorn to bring his troops east to help stop the Yankee advance on Corinth. This was so much wishful thinking. Van Dorn's army was in no shape to begin a four-hundred-mile march, and, in any case, the Union army would force Johnston's hand long before the Arkansas force could arrive.

---

44 William L. Shea and Earl J. Hess, *Pea Ridge: Civil War Campaign in the West* (Chapel Hill and London: University of North Carolina Press, 1992), 265 – 267.

## CHAPTER TEN

# Shiloh

*L*ate on the evening of April 2, word of Union movements west of Pittsburg Landing convinced Confederate Generals Beauregard and Johnston that Grant might be dividing his forces. This, they decided, was their chance to attack the forces remaining near the river before General Buell and the troops from Nashville could arrive. With any luck, they might even be able to match the Yankees' numbers. On Thursday morning, April 3, the Confederate camps were alive with drum rolls, bugle calls, and all the activity that it takes to get an army on the march.

It was only fifteen miles or so from Corinth north to the area where the Confederate troops would assemble to begin the battle. Unfortunately, organizing the various units and then marching over forty thousand men, plus horses, mules, wagons, and artillery pieces to their places using only two small country roads, which were quickly turned to mush by rain and the passage of thousands and thousands of feet, hooves, and wheels, took much longer than expected, and upset General Johnston's timetable. Johnston had ordered the attack to begin on Saturday morning, April 5, but his troops were far from ready.

It took all that day just to get the Confederates into position, and some of the senior officers were convinced that the element of surprise had been so compromised that the attack should be cancelled. They couldn't believe so much activity, virtually under the Yankees' noses, could have gone unnoticed. General Johnston, knowing that it was now or never, disagreed, commenting that "I would fight them if they were a million."[45] In fact, the Union commanders did pick up information of movement all across their front, but no one on the Yankees' side could bring themselves to believe that the Confederates were actually preparing to attack.

On Sunday morning, April 6, life began as usual in the Union camps around a little Methodist meeting house called Shiloh Church, just south of Pittsburg Landing. The men of General Sherman's command were building campfires, boiling coffee, and cooking breakfast when solid lines of Confederate troops came out of the woods toward them. So began the largest battle in the history of the Republic, up to that time.

At first, the totally surprised Yankees simply dropped everything and ran for their lives. However, given the number of men involved, spread out over an almost three-mile front, confusion soon became the order of the day. The Confederates, although sweeping the Yankees before them, began to have trouble keeping their units together, some stopping to rummage through abandoned Yankee camps. Also, before long, Union units began to recover from the initial shock and form pockets of resistance. All this took time, and that worked against the Confederates. By 10:00 a.m., many of the Union units were fighting back, and for the rest of the day, desperate, bloody encounters occurred all along the line at places that would soon become famous as the Sunken Road, Bloody Pond, the Peach Orchard, and the Hornet's Nest.

---

45 Foote, *The Civil War*, 329. The Confederates' problems assembling for the battle, the discussion about canceling the attack, and Johnston's quote are found in this source.

About 2:00 p.m., General Johnston, on his horse named Fire Eater, was riding near the fighting with some of his staff when he was hit by a bullet behind his right knee. The wound was partially covered by his high top riding boots, but it had torn his right popliteal artery. Johnston had earlier sent his personal physician to care for some wounded men, and no one in the general's party thought to apply the tourniquet which the general carried in his pocket, and which might have saved his life. Within half an hour, the Confederate commander bled to death on the field, and command passed to General P.G.T. Beauregard.[46] All these things had given General Grant enough time to assemble a last line of defense, near the riverbank.

Late in the afternoon, Grant and his subordinates managed to organize a number of retreating units, along with forty-one pieces of artillery, and position them to protect the landing on the river. Then, at 5:00 p.m., Grant received his best news all day. The first units of General Buell's army, marching from Nashville, came on the field, having appeared on the opposite bank of the Tennessee River earlier in the day and been ferried across to shore up Grant's defenses. Even so, fear still reigned in much of the Union army. Between 10,000 and 15,000 soldiers, who had thrown down their weapons, were crowded at the water's edge, hoping to escape, and the newly arriving troops had to force their way through the crowd of deserters to get to their positions. In spite of being forced back by the Confederate troops all day, when night fell on the battlefield, Grant's army remained in possession of the vital river landing.

General Beauregard, now in command of the Confederate forces, spent Sunday night in a tent that, twelve hours before, had belonged to

---

46 Welsh, *Medical Histories*, 118-119.

Union Gen. William T. Sherman. On Monday morning, however, he woke to a new reality. The newly reinforced Union army attacked, and by nightfall had retaken all the ground they had lost the previous day. It was now the Confederate army that was in retreat and confusion. There was some skirmishing on Tuesday, but by and large, General Grant was content to let the Southerners retreat back to Corinth.

The Battle of Shiloh has been called the first battle of modern warfare. It marked the end of the first year of the Civil War and gave both sides a glimpse of what was to come. In just over thirty-six hours, it produced more American casualties than had been suffered in all the previous wars in the nation's history. Of the 111,500 men listed by both sides as present for duty, over 23,000—about 21%—were either killed, wounded, or missing in action.[47]

Burton Warfield and his friends in the Second Battalion, Tennessee Cavalry could count themselves lucky that they missed the slaughter. They were on a scouting mission near Lawrenceburg, Tennessee, at the time, tracking the rest of Buell's army which was strung out for miles between there and Savannah.[48]

---

47 The Battle of Shiloh is well documented in many accounts. The above account comes from information contained in Shelby Foote's work and especially the excellent account of the battle by Larry Daniel, both cited previously.

48 T. H. Williams, *The Tennessee Civil War Questionnaires*, compiled by G. W. Dyer and J. T. Moore (Easley, SC: Southern Historical Press), Vol. 5, 2205-2207.

## CHAPTER ELEVEN

# Northern Mississippi

As the Confederate army retreated back into the area surrounding Corinth, Mississippi, and began to pull itself together after losing over 10,000 men, the Union Department Commander, Gen. Henry W. Halleck, went to Pittsburg Landing and took command of the Union forces personally. Halleck was better known in the Union army as a scholar than as a fighter. His nickname was "Old Brains." He was also "Old School," so instead of aggressively following on Beauregard's heels into Corinth, he began an advance that was totally "by the book," and so slow that it was described by men on both sides as "glacial." Slow or not, the Union troops outnumbered the Southerners almost two to one, so it was clear that the fall of Corinth was only a matter of time. Time, however, was what General Beauregard desperately needed, and Halleck gave it to him.

Early in May 1862, as part of a reorganization following the Battle of Shiloh, Burton Warfield's Second Battalion, Tennessee Cavalry was combined with the Eleventh Battalion from the same state to form the First Tennessee Cavalry Regiment [later to be officially designated the Sixth Tennessee Cavalry Regiment (Wheeler)]. When Corinth was finally evacuated during the night of May 29, this new unit was actually cut off by the Yankees, but managed to fight its way back to Confederate lines. On June 12, they were reorganized again and elected a new commanding officer, Col. James T. Wheeler.[49] It was probably during this time that Burton Warfield was elected First Lieutenant of Company "A" in the new First Tennessee Cavalry, second in command to Capt. G. M. V. Kinzer. Even though there are no surviving letters from this time, it is almost certain that Burton saw some real fighting. He and his unit would remain in northern Mississippi for the rest of 1862 and see at least two more major engagements and several smaller skirmishes.

Although there are no letters from Burton or Anna during this period, there is a letter written to Anna by her niece. Burton's older sister Henrietta had married Robert Reaves in 1837, and they had a daughter whom they named Alabama. In 1862, Bama Reaves was seventeen years old and living with her parents at Charlotte, Tennessee, about forty miles north of Anna's home. In her letter, it is obvious that Bama kept up with the latest news on the war as best she could, and considered herself quite the grown up, cultured, and loyal young Southern lady. At the end, she even added a little verse of poetry.

—⁂—

*Charlotte, Tennessee*

*June 19, 1862*

*Dear Anna*

> *Again I have seated myself to write you a few lines and by reading*

---

49 Lindsley, *Military Annals*, 2:885. On September 12, 1862, the Confederate Inspector General's office notified the unit that it already had a First Tennessee Cavalry Regiment on its books, and ordered it to be listed as the Sixth Tennessee Cavalry Regiment. The unit, however, and indeed, the rest of the army, continued to refer to itself as the First Tennessee Cavalry throughout the rest of the war, and mustered out in May, 1865, as such. This caused a lot of confusion in the records, and the regiment is variously referred to as the First Tennessee; the Second Tennessee, a throwback to its Second Battalion days; and—correctly—as the Sixth Tennessee Cavalry (Wheeler), referring to its commander, Col. James T. Wheeler.

*you will know that we are all well and frighten to death because we can hear nothing but Yankies. We have had several yanks to come down from Nashville to see us. Aunt Anna, did you hear Gen. Butler's proclamation, and is it not one of the most rediculious things you ever heard of, and is it no more sin to speak what you think than to think from the heart and not speak. So I would be glad to know that he, Gen Butler, was dead and buried so deep that the Lord could not find him at the resurrection day for I fear he will be cast off anyhow and as to being buried so deep, it is none to deep for one who has little respect for the ladies if they are in favor of the South, which I expect to be the longest day I live and any man of the South who claims to have Southern principles that would stand or sit and hear this proclamation and see how the North is going to disgrace the ladies of the Southern states and not go and fight in their defence, I and every other Southern lady will say he has no mark of a gentleman about him. And a man that will not go out to defend his home and friends, let him ask himself the question—what am I in the soldiers and ladies eyes? And his answer will be—why, I am an outcast and a disgrace to my country. Will it not bring any man to disgrace to think that he does not love his country no better than that. Ah, what cowards, what cowards. If I study anymore about this, I will not sleep a wink tonight.[50] But this must come. Well, it is said that the "Old Boy" rote to Beauregard a note and told him not to kill anymore Yankies—that hell was so full now that he did not have room for*

---

50 The subject of Miss Reaves' anger was Union Gen. Benjamin Butler (also known as "Spoons" because of his rumored fondness for captured silverware) who was, at the time, the military governor of New Orleans. In an attempt to correct the discourteous behavior of the New Orleans ladies toward Yankee troops (one had emptied a chamber pot from an upstairs window on the head of the Union Naval Commander), General Butler issued an order that any woman of the town showing contempt of any Union soldier would be treated as a common prostitute plying her trade.

anymore—that he would have to wait until he stiewed them down. I must go to bed now—finish in the morn.

Goodby

June 20, 1862

Good morning, Aunt Anna

It is very cold this morn. and I am in a hurry. Cousin Abe will start soon—he is to take this letter to Williamsport. He is coming back again before long and I am going home with him and stay some time. I would go now but he has got some boarders and I will wait until they go away, which will be soon. We hear that our prisoners are exchanged. You know we are all glad. We hear that Biffle's Battalion was in the mountains. Mr. C. Oakley, he was discharged, just got home yesterday, a month ago today since he left the C-Gap. He says the boys are going to leave there. They are going to Ky. where they can get to fight. Oh, it did make them and all the southern soldiers so mad when they heard of Butler's "woman law."

Aunt Anna, it is time to quit. Cousin Abe has gone to catch his horse. Tell all Uncle Worley's family howdy for me—and please write soon to your friend and niece.

B. Reaves

To Anna –

Peace be around thee wherever thou rovest
May life be to thee one pleasant summer day
And all that thou wishest and all that thou lovest
Come smiling around thy sunny way.
Ala. Reaves

—⁂—

It is obvious from her letter that young Miss Reaves, like everyone else, followed the progress of the war as closely as she could. It's also obvious that, had she not been a proper Christian young lady, her language concerning General Butler and his insult to Southern womanhood would have been even stronger.

Meanwhile, following the retreat from Corinth and the reorganization of the regiment, the the First Tennessee Cavalry[51] became part of a cavalry brigade commanded by Brig. Gen. Frank Armstrong, under the overall command of Maj. Gen Sterling Price, who had finally arrived with his troops from northwest Arkansas. On September 20th, they were with Price at the Battle of Iuka, Mississippi, and on October 3-4, they fought with Price's Division at Corinth, the overall command of the army then having passed to Maj. Gen. Earl Van Dorn. During the retreat from Corinth, the First Tennessee Cavalry formed part of the rear guard as the beaten Confederates took up blocking positions at Holly Springs.[52]

For the next two and a half months, the battered Confederate army in northern Mississippi regrouped, refitted, argued over who was responsible for their present condition, and shivered in the cold as winter brought snow and ice storms.[53] General Van Dorn's handling of the army was harshly criticized, and he was reduced from command of

---

51 Sam R. Watkins, *Co. Aytch* (New York: Simon and Schuster, 1997). There was also a First Tennessee Infantry Regiment, composed of men from Maury County. The First Tennessee Infantry and the First Tennessee Cavalry often came across one another during the war and caught up on the news from back home, since most of the men knew each other. This book contains the best account of the First Tennessee Infantry and their encounters with the First Tennessee Cavalry.

52 Lindsley, *Military Annals*, 885.

53 Foote, *The Civil War*, 725. Between Iuka and Corinth, they had sustained about 5,000 casualties.

the army to that of a corps. Meanwhile, Union forces had moved in to fill the void left by the Confederates' withdrawal from northeast Mississippi. Much to everyone's relief, General "Old Brains" Halleck had returned to his headquarters, returning the command of the army in the field to Gen. Grant. By late November, he commanded almost 70,000 men and was ready to advance on Vicksburg from the north, having established a huge supply base at Holly Springs to support the troop movement.[54] Ironically, this would also provide a chance for Earl Van Dorn to retrieve his sagging reputation.

Naturally, Grant's activities in north Mississippi didn't go unnoticed by the Confederate commanders. They had been forced out of Holly Springs in early November, and when Grant began his move toward Vicksburg on December 1, they moved further back to Grenada. Outnumbered almost three to one, they were in no position to confront Grant head on, but at this dark time for the Southern cause in Mississippi, Burton Warfield and his unit were about to take part in one of the most successful cavalry raids of the war.

On December 17, as Grant approached the Confederate positions at Grenada, Earl Van Dorn, a major general now reduced to personally commanding only three brigades of cavalry, led his men over one hundred miles in three days, circling east and then north around the Union army. On December 20, Van Dorn and his troopers, including Burton's First Tennessee Cavalry, thundered out of the sunrise and overwhelmed the few defenders at Grant's immense Holly Springs supply depot, sixty miles behind enemy lines. Having subdued all opposition, they began to burn, destroy, or carry off everything in sight. Van Dorn

---

54 Peter Cozzens, *The Darkest Days of the War* (Chapel Hill and London: University of North Carolina Press, 1997), 309.

later claimed to have captured 1,500 prisoners, burned all the quarter-master stores, which he estimated at $1,500,000, and destroyed several trains. He and his command then returned, unmolested, to Grenada. Van Dorn's raid, combined with Forrest's destruction of rail lines further north in the Jackson, Tennessee, area, crippled Grant's supply lines and forced him to withdraw, relieving the pressure on Vicksburg until spring.

Burton might, or might not, have been on this raid. After the defeat at Corinth, he was sent back to Maury County to gather more men. His name appears as the enlisting officer on the records of several new First Tennessee Cavalry recruits who joined during November 1862, so it is uncertain whether he made it back to Mississippi in time to take part in the Holly Springs raid. Before long, however, Burton, along with his entire regiment, would be back in Middle Tennessee. In January 1863, Major General Van Dorn, his star shining a little more brightly after his success at Holly Springs, was transferred, along with almost 6,000 troopers, including Burton's regiment, to Columbia, Tennessee.[55]

---

55 Ibid., 322.

## CHAPTER TWELVE

# Back Home in Maury County

The situation in Middle Tennessee had been more or less static since the beginning of the year. Following the battle of Murfrees-boro, on the evening of January 3, 1863, General Braxton Bragg began a retreat southward, setting up his new headquarters at Tullahoma. Union Gen. William Rosecrans remained in Murfreesboro, and there matters had stood for almost two months. Finally arriving in Columbia, Tennessee, in late February, Van Dorn was to command the cavalry on the left, or western, end of the Confederate line, which stretched almost seventy-five miles, from Van Dorn's position east through Shelbyville and Manchester to McMinnville. Along with his three brigades, Van Dorn would also have about two thousand other cavalry under Gen. Nathan Bedford Forrest, the prickly, but often brilliant former Memphis slave dealer who had only recently been transferred to Van Dorn's command after a serious falling out with his former commander.

Forrest was a rich forty-one-year-old plantation owner and busi-nessman with no formal military training, but a street fighter's instincts for what would—and would not—work in the field. Coming from the civilian world, Forrest often had problems with the military chain of command and showed little patience for those he considered incom-petent, regardless of rank. Joseph Wheeler was a twenty-six-year-old Regular Army man, just three years out of West Point when he was promoted over Forrest (as brigadiers, Forrest ranked Wheeler by three months) to major general in January 1863.[56]

On February 3, Forrest, under Wheeler's command, had lost several men and had two horses shot from under him in an engagement at Dover, Tennessee. Forrest had thought the attack ill conceived from the first and minced no words saying as much to his commander. Afterward, he told General Wheeler, who outranked him, but was fifteen years younger, to include in his official report to General Bragg the statement that "I [Forrest] will be in my coffin before I will fight again under your [Wheeler's] command." Even though often insubordinate and abrasive, Forrest had already become indispensable when the shooting started, so Wheeler, who actually admired the fiery cavalryman, gave him his wish and arranged his transfer to Van Dorn, which suited Forrest just fine.[57]

Van Dorn's job was to use his cavalry to harass the Union troops and attack their supply lines in the area from Columbia northward all the way to Nashville, if possible, and just over a week after his arrival, the Yankees played right into his hands.

On March 3, the Federal commander at Franklin was ordered to send a brigade, along with artillery and cavalry support, down the Columbia Pike toward Spring Hill. They were to reconnoiter in that direction and link up with another force, already on the road from Murfreesboro under Phil Sheridan, expected to arrive in the area on March 5. The plan was to combine forces and then move on toward Columbia with its vital bridge over the Duck River. News—or at least

---

56 Welsh, *Medical Histories*, 71, 232.
57 Jack Hurst, *Nathan Bedford Forrest: A Biography* (New York: Alfred A. Knopf, 1993), 114.

rumor—of Van Dorn's arrival must have reached Union Headquarters, because General Rosecrans' requirements were made clear at the end of the order:"We desire to know what is in our front."[58]

At 9:00 a.m. the next morning, Col. John Coburn marched out of Franklin with five regiments of infantry (1,845 men), 600 cavalry, and one artillery battery, a total of 2,837 troops. Only four miles south of Franklin, Coburn's lead units ran into Confederate skirmishers who were the advance party of General Van Dorn's troops, coming up from Spring Hill. There was sporadic fighting for several hours, but the day ended with Coburn encamped on Columbia Pike about two miles or so north of Thompson's Station, a settlement of a few houses around a depot on the Tennessee and Alabama Railroad. Convinced that there was a substantial enemy force in front of them, the Union soldiers slept on their arms that night.

Everyone was up bright and early on the morning of March 5, with Coburn's troops on the road marching south again by 8:00 a.m. Unfortunately for John Coburn, just south of Thompson's Station, Earl Van Dorn waited with almost 6,000 men. The resulting battle went badly for the Indiana colonel, especially since, in the middle of the fighting, some of his infantry and all his cavalry and artillery units decided, on their own, to retreat back toward Franklin. In the end, Coburn and what was left of his command surrendered and were taken prisoner— 1,221 men. By March 21, Coburn and all his men, except those who died on the way, were in Libby Prison in Richmond.[59] At this time, however, the north was still exchanging prisoners, so their stay at Libby Prison

---

58 Frank J. Welcher and Larry G. Ligget, *Coburn's Brigade* (Carmel, IN: Guild Press of Indiana, 1999), 51.
59 Ibid., 55-69, 92.

was short, but very unpleasant. Lt. J. N. Hill, Company "E," Thirty-Third Indiana, wounded at Thompson's Station, later wrote home: "I was in Libby only about three weeks, and ten more days would have ended my life. I was worn out and starved. My flesh was all wasted away, and lice literally swarmed all over me. The surgeon on board the vessel at City Point said the lice would have killed me in another week if nothing else had been the matter."[60] Fortunately, the first of Coburn's men were exchanged on April 1, with all the rest following by the fifteenth.

Burton's unit was present at this battle, listed under the correct designation of Sixth Tennessee Cavalry regiment, part of Gen. Frank Armstrong's brigade, but may not have played much of a part. It is said to have arrived on the field as the battle was ending.

The following letter was written to a member of the Ninth Tennessee Cavalry, which had many men from Maury County. The Ninth Tennessee (also known as the 19th Tn Cav) was commanded by Burton's former commander in the old Second Battalion, Col. J. B. Biffle, and certainly did see action at Thompson's Station and several other places under General Forrest. The letter was written by Mary Worley Brooks, Anna Worley Warfield's older sister, to her husband, Thomas Brantley Brooks, who was Burton's nephew as well as his brother-in-law. Although written only one day after the engagement at Thompson's Station, the first part of the letter may indicate that Mrs. Brooks, who lived within twenty-five miles of the place, had already heard news of the battle. More likely, though, it refers to some earlier engagement her husband told her about.

—⁂—

---

60 Ibid., 94.

*March 6th '63*

*Dear Tom*

    *I again seat myself to write you a few lines to let you know that we are all well, although I am well in body I am much affected in mind on account of the critical position in which you are all placed. I was very sorry indeed that you was rushed toward the enemy without being better drilled but we must put our trust in him who rides on high and guards the steps of his children. Bill told me that you was about getting swapped into Kinzer's company.[61] I have nothing to say to that but let your own judgment decide. I was very glad to hear from you on Sunday last but was much disappointed Saturday evening when you did not come home. I was satisfied that something had happened to prevent your coming. I was told before I read your letter that you said you did not intend coming nohow, that you had been home one night and that would do, but you know I did not believe one word of that. I want you to come home as soon as you can. Be sure and keep out of range of the Yankee bullets and do not let them catch you if you can help it. John Runions said he did not know whether he could take your place or not but I think if you could ever get settled, I could persuade him to go awhile.*

    *The children all want to see you very bad. Lonny calls for you almost every day. You remember what I told you when you was at home? I am sorry to inform you that it is all too true but I will bear up as well as I can. I would be glad if you would all make peace and come home. I believe I have written every thing that I can think of now and will excuse my bad*

---

61 Brooks seems to have been trying to transfer from the Ninth Tennessee Cavalry to the Sixth Tennessee Cavalry, which makes sense. "Kinzer's company" was almost certainly Co. "A," Sixth Tennessee Cavalry, commanded by Capt. G. M. V. Kinzer, a neighbor, with Brooks' brother-in-law and uncle Burton Warfield as First Lieutenant.

*Tom Brooks, Private, Company E, 19th Tennessee Calvary (Biffle's) circa 1863.*
*Photo courtesy of Laura Hayes, Hampshire, TN,*
*Tom Brooks' great-great granddaughter.*

*writing for Lonny is playing over my back and I cannot half write. Be sure and write soon and come home as soon as you can get a half a chance.*

*Nothing more but remains as ever yours.*

*Mary*[62]

Note: Mary Brooks, at this time, had three children at home, Alice, seven years old, Ella, four, and Lonnie, almost two (who was "playing over my back"). In the last paragraph, she tells her husband Tom that the thing she told him about "is all too true." The "thing" was the fact that she was pregnant again. Mary Anna Brooks was born at the end of October. No wonder she wished "you would all make peace and come home."

—◊◊◊—

Having spoiled the Yankees' raid, Van Dorn next planned one of his own, led by General Forrest. Three weeks after the affair at Thompson's Station, Forrest rode north out of Spring Hill with six cavalry regiments and a few other smaller units to attack a Union force at Brentwood, Tennessee. Skirting the Union fortifications at Franklin, two regiments went east of the town, while Forrest led the remainder of the force to the west and then north on Hillsboro Pike. By 7:00 a.m. on March 25, Forrest had turned back east and was overlooking the Federal works at Brentwood. He immediately sent a message, under a flag of truce, asking for their surrender, but the Michigan and Wisconsin men declined. After a short skirmish, however, they had a change of heart and struck their colors. They turned out to be led by a Lieutenant Colonel Bloodgood, the same officer who had escaped capture at Thompson's Station by leading about 150 men of the Twenty-Second Wisconson in a hasty retreat. Ironically—some said deservedly—Bloodgood would now follow his old commander

---

62 *Historic Maury*, Vol. 5 No. 1, 2-8 & No. 2, 27-31.

to Libby Prison, arriving only a week after his former comrades in Coburn's Brigade.[63]

Leaving most of his force to deal with the 520 or so prisoners, their arms, and provisions, Forrest then took two brigades and some artillery about two miles south where he found 230 men in a stockade guarding a railroad bridge over the Little Harpeth River. One shot from a field piece convinced the defenders there to surrender, also. As soon as the bridge was set on fire and the prisoners rounded up, the Confederates withdrew to the west, back toward Hillsboro Pike, taking everything they could carry.

In this engagement, Burton's Sixth Tennessee Cavalry was given a special assignment by General Forrest himself. This is the only time we have an official account of an action in which Burton Warfield was involved, as well as his personal account of the same action, given in a letter to his wife. Lt. Col. James H. Lewis was commanding the Sixth Tennessee Cavalry on this occasion, since Colonel Wheeler was still recovering from wounds received at Holly Springs. What follows is a transcript of Lewis' official report of the action to his brigade commander, Brig. Gen. Frank Armstrong, CSA, and then Burton's personal account, given in a letter to Anna, dated one day earlier.

—m—

*Report of Lieut. Col. James H Lewis, First* [Sixth] *Tennessee Cavalry*
*March 28, 1863*

*GENERAL: In obedience to orders received, I have the honor to forward to you a report of the part taken by the regiment under my command at Brentwood and around Nashville.*

*We were not engaged with the enemy at Brentwood, but were present*

---

63 Welcher, *Coburn's Brigade*, 80.

at the capture. *Immediately after the enemy's surrender, I was ordered by Adjutant and Inspector General* [Assistant Adjutant General] [Samuel M.] *Hyams jr. to report to you, which I did, and by your order reported to General* [N. B.] *Forrest, who directed me to move rapidly in the direction of Nashville from Brentwood; if possible, capture a lot of 150 negroes, and other property I might find that belonged to the enemy, and drive in their pickets, &c. I moved rapidly in the direction of Nashville; their pickets had been alarmed, and on our approach fled. A portion of the regiment galloped up within 2 ½ or 3 miles of Nashville, in plain view of the enemy's encampment near the city; captured a sutler of One hundred and thirteenth Ohio, 1 two-horse wagon and team and 10 negroes, who were in possession of the enemy. I then moved across to the Charlotte Pike, making half the circuit of Nashville across the different turnpike roads, at a distance of 3 ½ to 5 miles of Nashville; had a plain view of the city and capitol, and moved down the Charlotte turnpike to a point 8 miles from Nashville, near the Cumberland River, where I remained from 3 p.m. until 9 p.m., momentarily expecting the arrival of yourself with General Forrest, who had informed me that they would certainly come to that point. Hearing nothing from you, I moved off at 9 p.m. and arrived here yesterday, 27th instant, with all the property captured. No loss to the regiment, except the bad condition of horses.*

*I have the honor to be, your obedient servant,*

*Jas. H. Lewis*

*Lieutenant Colonel, Commanding First* [Sixth] *Tennessee Cavalry.*

*Brigadier General* [Frank C.] *Armstrong,*

*Commanding First Cavalry Brigade.*[64]

---

64 *War of the Rebellion: A Compilation of the Official Records of the Union and Confederate Armies*, Vol. XXXV, 191.

—⁓—

The following letter was written by 1st Lt. Burton Warfield, Company "A," First [Sixth] Tennessee Cavalry, to his wife Anna, following the Brentwood Raid.

—⁓—

*Camp 1st Tenn Cav near Spring* (Hill)
*March 27* [1863]
*Dear Anna*

We have just returned from a raid on Brentwood near Nashville. We were gone four days traveled day and night. I have not slept more than four hours in the time. I am so sleepy I can hardly hold my eyes open. But we had a very good time withall. We captured about seven hundred Yankies and a good many negros. A good many of the boys got in the Fed Camps at Brentwood several things but we were ordered on the Pike towards Nashville to capture some negros near Nashville. We went within 2 miles of Nashville captured some negros and would have taken thirty or forty wagons but were ordered back just as we got in sight of them. We were afraid the Yanks would get in our rear. We then went across to the Charlott Pike in 3 1/2 miles of Nashville. We went to the Cumberland and saw several transports. The prisoners we captured were sent off immediately. They passed through Williamsport yesterday or this morning. I wish you could have seen them. Lonny did not go with us from Brentwood. He staid there some time and got several little tricks some of which he is going to send home by Bill in the morning. Make Bill show them to you. Bill has a little port folio for you but it has nothing in it. The boys got some that were full of papers and envelopes and other nice little tricks. I don't know how long we will remain here. I will try and come home before we leave here again. I am much fatigued from our trip. We have been advance guard and rear guard the whole time and last night I was on picket. I was *nearer home yesterday than I am now. I saw one of my old sweet hearts today. Bettie Dodson of Santa Fe. She used to…[illegible]. I am verry well considering the bad weather. I want to sleep some to night. I am near the land of nod now. I can buy plenty of tobacco here for 12 1/2 cents [for] five large twists. But I have quit smoking—have not smoked but once for a week that was this morning to keep from going to sleep. You must write to me by Bill. Tell him to come by when he comes back here. I will try and come home myself soon. give my love to all*

*As ever yours,*

*Burton*

—⚏—

Burton and his fellow troopers may have gotten a few days rest after they got back to their camps near Spring Hill, but General Van Dorn was intent on keeping up the pressure in his area. On April 10 there was a sharp engagement at Franklin in which Burton's unit, again attached to General Forrest's command, had one man killed and four wounded. General Forrest was at the head of the Confederate column moving north on the Lewisburg Road, a few miles south of Franklin, when the rear of the column—Gen. Frank Armstrong's brigade, which included Burton's unit—was attacked by Union cavalry under Gen. David Stanley. As Armstrong prepared to counterattack, he sent a courier forward to General Forrest, apprising him of this disaster in the making. "General Stanley has cut in behind you, has captured the rearguard battery and many prisoners, and has now got into General Armstrong's rear!" the courier said. What followed was pure, vintage Forrest.

Shouting loud enough for the troops to hear, Forrest replied, "You say he is in Armstrong's rear? That's where I've been trying to get him all day, damn him! I'll be in his rear in about five minutes. Face your line of battle about. Armstrong, push forward your skirmish line. Crowd 'em both ways. I'll go to the rear brigade, and you'll hear from me there directly." Even though he had been surprised and was in a precarious position, he had already won the battle for his men's morale. Forrest's outburst convinced all the troops who heard him that the Yankees had actually fallen into his trap! A few minutes later, General Forrest led a charge which broke up the Union attack.[65]

Riding with Nathan Bedford Forrest, the finest and most successful cavalry commander produced by either side during the Civil War, was certainly exciting as well as exhausting, but the April 10 action is probably the last time Burton had the honor. On April 23, Forrest was ordered to northern Alabama to help deal with a force of Union raiders led by Col. Able Streight, leaving the area south of Nashville to Van Dorn and his original troops, including Burton's unit. By the time Forrest returned, Van Dorn would be gone, a victim of his own indiscretion.

---

65 Hurst, *Nathan Bedford Forrest*, 115-116.

## CHAPTER THIRTEEN
# *One Too Many Buggy Rides*

I n addition to being an ambitious soldier, Earl "Buck" Van Dorn was also well known as a lady's man. At forty-two years of age, Van Dorn still cut quite a dashing figure, and even though a married man, his attentions to the fair sex, married or single, were not always unwelcome. In the social atmosphere of Spring Hill, Tennessee, in the spring of 1863, he caught the eye of the young wife of a prominent doctor. From later accounts, the attraction was entirely mutual. Her name was Jessie Helen McKissack Peters.

Jessie, twenty-four years younger than her husband, was the third wife of Dr. George B. Peters, a wealthy man who owned property in Tennessee and Arkansas. Described as "an incredibly beautiful woman" and a "beguiling temptress," her unsupervised visits to the general's office caused such a stir that Dr. White, the owner of the house, ask Van Dorn to relocate his headquarters. This he promptly did, moving into the Martin Cheairs home at the end of April.

Dr. Peters, no longer a practicing physician, had been in West Tennessee and Arkansas for nearly a year. During this year, some local citizens describe the vivacious Jessie as being "just plain lonesome." Nonetheless, Van Dorn's late night visits to the Peters' home and the couple's long, un-chaperoned carriage rides became common knowledge. It was inevitable that the general's ungentlemanly conduct would be found out by the man with whose wife he was enjoying a dalliance.

According to Dr. Peters' own testimony, he had finally decided to take the oath of allegiance to the United States while in Memphis. Claiming he had done it to obtain protection for his Arkansas property, on April 4, 1863, he received a pass through the Federal lines to return home. In his own words, Peters stated, "I arrived at home on the 12th of April and was alarmed at the distressing rumors which prevailed in the neighborhood in relation to the attentions paid by General Van Dorn to my wife." Peters also claimed to have intercepted one of Van Dorn's servants delivering a note to Jessie and told him to "tell his whiskey-headed master, General Van Dorn, that I would blow his brains out, or any of his staff that stepped their foot inside of the lawn." None of this seems to have cooled Van Dorn's ardor, for the doctor later said that he faked a trip out of town only to return unexpectedly and catch the general and his wife *in flagrante delicto.*[66]

A situation like this could only come to a bad end, and on the morning of May 7, Dr. Peters entered the Cheairs home near Spring Hill, which General Van Dorn used as a headquarters, entered the general's private office, and shot him in the head. Dr. Peters escaped across the lines into Federal territory, and Van Dorn died a few hours later, never regaining consciousness.

Some say that Dr. Peters had other, more political motives for killing Van Dorn besides the affair with his wife, but the dashing Confederate general was just as dead, whatever the cause. Burton Warfield's regiment, the Sixth Tennessee Cavalry, escorted Van Dorn's remains to the

---

66 Alethea Sayers, "Road to Dishonor." Available online at *http://www.civilwarweb.com* in 2004. "Ms. Sayers additionally credited: "The Generals Tour" by David Roth, *Blue & Gray,* Oct.-Nov.1984, and "Earl Van Dorn," by Albert Castel, *Civil War Times Illustrated,* April 1967.

*Ferguson Hall, Spring Hill, TN, home of Martin Cheairs and site of the murder of General Earl Van Dorn. Photo from author's collection.*

cemetery at Columbia, but he was later re-interred at Port Gibson, Mississippi.[67]

The situation in Middle Tennessee—and therefore the situation of Burton Warfield's unit—remained the same for the rest of May and most of June. Following General Van Dorn's death, the command fell to General Forrest who, upon his return from Alabama, continued to raid and generally harass the Union forces in his area. On June 13, however, Forrest himself was shot by a disgruntled junior officer who felt that Forrest had questioned his courage on the battlefield. The general survived the attack, but Lt. A. W. Gould did not. After being shot in the left side, Forrest fatally stabbed Lieutenant Gould with his penknife. Such were the exciting goings-on in the Confederate forces of which Burton was a part. On the Union side, the drama was taking place at a much higher level.

---

67 Lindsley, *Military Annals*, 887 and Welch, *Medical Histories*, 221.

CHAPTER FOURTEEN
## *Breaking the Stalemate*

A t the beginning of the new year, 1863, the Union commander in Middle Tennessee, Maj. Gen. William S. Rosecrans, was one of the few bright lights in an otherwise gloomy outlook for the Northern war effort. Two weeks before Christmas, the Army of the Potomac's new but reluctant commander, Ambrose Burnside, had marched on Fredericksburg, Virginia, with 120,000 men to meet Gen. Robert E. Lee who fielded only two-thirds as many troops. The Union threw most of their strength at the Confederate positions along Marye's Heights, south of the town, and lost over 12,000 men within a few hours. Most of them went against a position held by Gen. James Longstreet, whose men inflicted 9,000 casualties without a single Yankee soldier reaching the Confederate line. Prior to the battle, Longstreet had asked his artillery commander if he needed any more guns to cover the approaches to his position. The artilleryman declined, saying that he already covered the ground so well that, in his words, "a chicken could not live on that field when we open on it." As it turned out, he was very nearly right.[68]

Rosecrans, on the other hand, met his opposite number, Braxton Bragg, at Murfreesboro, Tennessee, on the last day of 1862, on almost

---

68 Foote, *The Civil War*, 22.

even terms, and after three days remained in possession of the field, while his opponent retreated. The fact that Rosecrans, with far fewer troops at Murfreesboro, actually suffered more casualties than the disgraced Burnsides did at Fredericksburg was largely overlooked in Washington. "Old Rosey" was a winner, and that was what mattered most. Five months later, however, when he was still sitting in the same place, Rosecrans' star had dimmed considerably, and some in the Capitol were calling for his head. By the middle of June, he received an ultimatum from his superiors: either move on Bragg or be replaced. Finally, at 3:00 a.m. on June 24, Rosecrans began the offensive he had been planning since January, and it would determine Burton Warfield's fate for the next two years.

Rosecrans' offensive was meticulously planned and complicated— just the type of plan that often spelled disaster since it required coordination between units, which was often difficult or even impossible to achieve once the battle started. This time, though, Rosecrans' delay and attention to detail paid off. For one of the few times in the Civil War, a battle went even better than its commander had envisioned. By the next day, Bragg and his troops were in full retreat toward Chattanooga.

The collapse of the Confederate line in Middle Tennessee changed everything for Burton's unit and the others stationed near Columbia. General Forrest immediately took most of his troops east to help screen Bragg's men as they fell back toward the Tennessee River, but a few were left in the Columbia area for various reasons. Some were required to guard the supply wagons. For months, Confederate quartermasters had been scouring Middle Tennessee for supplies to keep Bragg's men and animals fed, and the effort continued, even during the retreat. Recruiting efforts also continued. For these and other reasons, small bodies of Confederate soldiers remained in and around Columbia and Maury County for several weeks after the main body of the army was gone.

The Union army paid little attention to the area, being occupied with its pursuit of the main force to the southeast, so the few Confederate soldiers who stayed near Columbia actually enjoyed a relatively peaceful few weeks. Of course, it couldn't last.

# CHAPTER FIFTEEN
## *The Lightning Brigade*

*T*he first days of July, 1863, leading up to the eighty-seventh anniversary of the Declaration of Independence, were an anxious but ultimately glorious time for President Lincoln and the Union. Although it would take a few days for the word to spread, two momentous events—separated by almost a thousand miles—had just taken place. During the first three days of the month, Union forces under George Meade had, in what remains the largest battle ever fought in North America, defeated Robert E. Lee at Gettysburg, Pennsylvania, and forced his Army of Northern Virginia back south of the Potomac. Then, on July 4, Gen. U. S. Grant accepted the surrender of the Confederate forces at Vicksburg, giving the North control of the Mississippi River over its entire length. All this good news, however, failed to lift the spirits of one Union officer in Middle Tennessee.

Col. James Monroe, the former mayor of Mattoon, Illinois, was worn out in body and distressed in mind as he sat in his tent near Wartrace. While others slept or celebrated the holiday, Monroe was writing a letter to his commander, resigning as colonel of the 123rd Illinois Infantry Regiment. He had been fighting for two years; his health was broken; his father-in-law, to whom he had entrusted his affairs back home, had recently died; his business was in decline; and the bank had recently foreclosed on his house. If he was to salvage anything of his property for his family's future, he wrote, he must go home. On hearing of his letter, his immediate commander, Colonel Wilder of the First Brigade, Fourth Division, Fourteenth Army Corps, Union Army of the Cumberland, told him that he was too valuable to lose and gave him another assignment. A few days later, Colonel Monroe and his men would change the course of Burton and Anna Warfield's life.[69]

Col. John T. Wilder, Monroe's brigade commander, was a capable and innovative officer. Not long after bringing his unit to Tennessee, in December 1862, he began working to put in place two major changes which would radically alter the character of his unit. First, Wilder proposed to turn his unit into a Mounted Infantry Brigade. General Rosecrans liked the idea, but doubted that the army could provide the mounts and forage. No problem, Wilder told his boss, and sent his men out across the countryside, rounding up horses and mules wherever they could be found. The Union soldiers considered themselves to be foragers, but not surprisingly, the citizens across Middle Tennessee whose stock was taken saw them more as common horse thieves. Wilder's men persisted, however, and by late June, they were as mobile as most cavalry units, but his other innovation would make them much more lethal.[70]

Colonel Wilder had long wanted a more modern weapon for his troops than the standard issue single-shot muzzle loaders, and in late March 1863, he found it. After seeing a demonstration by Christopher Spencer of his new seven shot repeater, Wilder immediately set out to acquire them for his brigade. Again, not willing to depend on the Union army's supply system, he arranged private financing through his

---

69 Richard A. Baumgartner, *Blue Lightning* (Huntington, WV: Blue Acorn Press, 1997), 37, 55-56.
70 Ibid., 19ff.

bankers back in Indiana and ordered over two thousand Spencer Rifles and ammunition directly from the factory in Boston.[71] By the time General Rosecrans launched his offensive against Bragg's Confederate Army of the Tennessee, Wilder's Brigade was mounted and armed.

Even though this new "Mounted Infantry" concept was untried in combat, General George Thomas thought enough of Wilder's men to use them as the spearhead of his part of the Union offensive. Derisively called "tadpole cavalry" by no less than Rosecrans' own chief of cavalry, Wilder's two thousand men trotted off at 4:00 a.m. on June 24, in a steady rain, toward Hoover's Gap, one of three passes through the range of hills shielding the Confederates' position and General Thomas' primary objective in the overall plan.

Wilder's men were just supposed to open the way for the rest of Thomas' forces, but meeting only light resistance from a few skirmishers, they galloped on through to the southern end of the pass. There they deployed as infantry and with their new Spencer repeaters, held their position against the better part of a Confederate division for the next twelve hours, until the rest of Thomas' troops could arrive on foot. In this action, they lost only fourteen killed and forty-seven wounded—3% casualties at a time when 15 to 20% was not uncommon. When General Thomas arrived that evening, he told them that their action had saved a thousand lives, which was probably not an exaggeration since he had expected it to take three days to force Hoover's Gap. There was no more talk of "tadpole cavalry." The unit was henceforth to be known as "Wilder's Lightning Brigade" by General Thomas' special order.[72]

Ironically, Wilder's Brigade's fine performance on the first day of

---

71 Ibid., 33-34.
72 Ibid., 47-51.

the offensive earned them the right to ride and fight for six more days in the constant rain and mud before finally being sent to the rear, men worn out and mounts broken down. It was at the end of this action that Colonel Monroe of the 123rd Illinois decided to sit down and celebrate Independence Day by writing his resignation.

## CHAPTER SIXTEEN

# Captured

*"My fine mare went up when I did as a matter of corse."*[73] *(Burton Warfield)*

I t took a few days for Colonel Monroe's letter of July 4 to come to the attention of Colonel Wilder, and for it to be rejected. Instead of being allowed to resign, Colonel Monroe was informed that he would have the honor of leading a "scout" westward down the Duck River to sweep up any stray Rebels left behind during Bragg's retreat, and to "show the flag" in that area of the state formally under Confederate control.[74]

The entire brigade wouldn't be required, so it was only a few hundred men that left their campsites near Wartrace on Sunday morning, July 12, and moved toward Maury County, Tennessee. A day or two later, an advance force of seventy-five men, led by Maj. James A. Connolly, rode into the town square of Columbia, to the complete surprise of the local citizens and the Confederate troops still stationed there.[75] The

---

73 Quoted from a letter from Burton Warfield to his wife, describing the capture of himself and his prized mare.

74 Baumgartner, *Blue Lightning*, 56.

75 The actual date of the Union raid on Columbia, Tennessee, is in some dispute. A local man's diary (Nimrod Porter) gives the date of the raid as Monday, July 13. Letters of Major Connolly (cited in #76), the officer who led the advance party, however, seem to indicate that they left camp at Wartrace on Sunday, July 12, raided Lewisburg on Monday, the 13th, and Columbia "the next day," July 14. Except for one obvious error, all of Burton Warfield's records also give the date of his capture as July 14, 1863.

Rebels scattered in all directions, but thirty-three were captured, including three lieutenants. One of these officers remains unknown, but one of the others, Lt. A. O. P. Nicholson, Jr., was from a prominent local family, his father being a former United States senator, and his capture sparked one of Maury County's most famous Civil War stories.[76]

One of the witnesses to the capture of Lieutenant Nicholson was a fifteen-year-old girl named Antoinette Polk, the daughter of Andrew Polk, a local man operating as a Confederate blockade runner, and the niece of Confederate Lt. Gen. Leonidas Polk. While others panicked at the sudden appearance of Yankee troops and the capture of Lieutenant Nicholson, Miss Polk knew exactly what she must do. At Ashwood, her family home six miles south of town, more Confederate troops were quartered, and she was determined to warn them.

Antoinette saddled her horse, a fine Arabian named Shiloh, and set off for home, but was soon spotted by a group of mounted Yankees. For three miles, she led them on a merry chase through the countryside, jumping fences and hedgerows, and finally leaving their worn-out mounts far behind. All the Yankees managed to capture was her ostrich-plumed hat. Thanks to the brave young Southern Belle, the Confederate soldiers at Ashwood escaped, but early the next morning, Colonel Monroe arrived with the rest of his men. Despite Antoinette's pleas, they took Shiloh and one hundred head of other thoroughbred stock. Antoinette Polk lived another fifty-six years, moved to Europe, was presented to Queen Victoria at Buckingham Palace, married a French baron, and entertained American "Doughboys" at her estate during World War One, but she never forgave the Yankees for

---

76 James A. Connolly, *Transactions of the Illinois State Historical Society for the Year 1928* (Springfield: Phillips Bros. 1928), 274-275.

stealing her horse.[77]

As they left Columbia, Colonel Monroe and his men took along their prisoners, including the third officer captured the day before—1st Lt. Burton Warfield, Company "A," First Tennessee Cavalry.[78]

Two days later, Major Connolly was once again leading an advance party into Centerville, when he wounded and paroled Lt. Col. George Gantt, commander of the Ninth Battalion, Tennessee Cavalry. This was the same Colonel Gantt which Burton mentioned in an earlier letter, having heard that his unit was "cut to pieces" at Fort Donelson. Colonel Monroe and his small force were now eighty miles from their camp, and, hearing rumors of Confederate troops moving to intercept them, he decided to circle back to the south and return to his lines. He and his troops arrived back in their camp on July 18, bringing with them fifty to sixty prisoners, 250 to 300 "Negroes," and between 700 and 800 horses. All this was accomplished with the loss of only one man.[79]

---

77 The story of Miss Polk's heroic efforts to warn the Confederate soldiers stationed at her home comes from a Certificate of Authenticity that accompanies a limited edition print titled "Antoinette's Ride" by artist Lisa Pardon of Columbia, Tennessee, July, 1998.

78 Warfield Official Records.

79 Baumgartner, *Blue Lightning,* 56. The numbers vary, depending on the source.

*Burton Warfield 1st Lt. Company "A" 1st Tennessee Cavalry*
*circa 1863*
*Picture courtesy of Loreace Concannon, wife of Burton Warfield's grandson*
*George Concannon. Copy provided by Gary Concannon and Ted Sahd*

## Chapter Seventeen
### *Prisoner of War*

For all of recorded history, countries at war have had to deal with the problem of prisoners taken during battle. For some, they were actually an asset. For a Roman general like Julius Caesar or Pompey the Great, prisoners of war were an important source of income. To the victorious general went the privilege of selling his prisoners into slavery. Most Roman legions were accompanied by the general's personal slave broker for just this reason. Many prisoners also wound up as fodder for wild animals in the great games in Rome. Nineteen hundred years later, in "enlightened" America, the treatment of POWs should have been more humane, but as Burton was about to find out, for many reasons, some things never change.

In the months leading up to the beginning of the war, many on both sides clung to the hope that actual combat could be avoided, and even when the shooting started, the prevailing belief was that it would be a short affair. This attitude meant that both sides went into the war almost totally unprepared in many areas, including arrangements for dealing with the inevitable numbers of prisoners. When the prisoners began to come in, both sides found themselves "playing catch up" in providing the basic necessities of life.

The lot of a prisoner of war has always been a hard one, but several things made the Civil War prisoner's experience especially grim. The lack of preparation by both sides meant that prison facilities were makeshift at best and barbaric at worst. For a while, however, parole and exchange agreements, which allowed prisoners to be returned to their own lines, kept the population of POWs down to almost manageable levels. Unfortunately for Burton, this exchange cartel broke down just before he was captured, so he entered the Union prisoner of war system at a time when the numbers were beginning to climb rapidly.

The American Civil War eventually involved a number of combatants which was beyond the wildest estimates of those on either side in 1861. Before the war was over, 4.2 million men would serve in either Blue or Gray. Of this number, 674,000 would find themselves prisoners of war at some point—almost 16% of the total enlistment, more than in any other war, before or since. What is more revealing is that, according to the statistics, a soldier was actually safer in the army, even with the risk of disease and the possibility of combat, than in a prison camp—North or South. Only about 5% of the soldiers on both sides were killed in action, but of the men held in POW camps, the overall death rate was 13% - 15% for those in Confederate prisons and 12% for those in Union ones.[80] Having survived two years in the field as a cavalryman, Burton Warfield suddenly faced a bigger challenge—surviving the Union prison system.

From the Union camps around Wartrace and Shelbyville, Burton and his fellow prisoners were transferred, probably by rail, to Nashville and then on to Louisville, Kentucky, arriving on July 21, 1863. The prison at Louisville was located on Broadway between Tenth and Eleventh Streets, but was mainly used as a holding facility for prisoners bound

---

80 Lonnie R. Speer, *Portals to Hell: Military Prisons of the Civil War* (Mechanicsburg, PA: Stackpole Books, 1997), XIV, 341n5.

for other more permanent camps. Louisville was considered too close to the Confederate lines, so unless a prisoner was too sick or wounded to continue on, his stay in Kentucky would be brief. In fact, Burton stayed in Louisville almost three weeks, but on Sunday, August 9, he was loaded into a rail car, along with many other Confederates, mostly officers, and sent further north.

If he was lucky, Burton had a seat on a wooden bench in a passenger car and could watch as the lush farmland of Indiana and western Ohio went by. This time of the year, it would have been fields of corn, as far as he could see. If he was unlucky, he would have seen the same scenes through the slats in the side of a box car, jammed in with a hundred or so other men. Either way, the 275-mile trip took two days.

On Tuesday morning, August 11, Burton and his fellow prisoners were unloaded at the depot in Sandusky, Ohio, and marched through town to the jeers and taunts of the local crowd that always seemed to turn out for the trainloads of captured Rebels. At the dock at the foot of Columbus Street, they were loaded aboard a side-wheel steamer named the *Island Queen* for the last three miles of the trip. Across Sandusky Bay, just before it opened up into Lake Erie, Burton could see a low, wooded island, which would be his home for the next eight months.[81]

---

81 Roger Long, "Johnson's Island Prison," *Blue and Gray*, March, 1987, 6ff.

## Chapter Eighteen
### *Johnson's Island*

B y the fall of 1861, both sides were beginning to realize that the war would be longer and harder fought than they first thought. Initially, the prisoners were exchanged or paroled or scattered around in whatever facilities were available, but now both governments began to try to bring some order to what had become a chaotic system.

In October, the Union army appointed Lt. Col. William Hoffman to run its prisoner of war operation, with instructions to survey the islands in Lake Erie and pick a location for a new POW camp, and on the north edge of Sandusky Bay, he found the perfect spot. Previously known as Bull Island, it was owned at the time by L. B. Johnson, who called it, modestly enough, "Johnson's Island." Hoffman quickly closed a deal to lease half the island for $500 a year, but once the camp was in place, the Army effectively controlled the entire three-hundred-acre site. Working through the winter, local contractors built the prison compound, and it accepted its first inmates—two hundred men from Camp Chase near Columbus, Ohio—on April 11, 1862.

If a person ended up as a Confederate prisoner in the spring of 1862, Johnson's Island was the best place to be. The lumber used to build the prisoners' barracks was green and left gaps in the walls when it dried, but that actually helped the ventilation in the summer, and winter was still months away. The food was relatively plentiful, if pretty basic, and if the prisoner had a little money, he could also buy fresh fruit and vegetables from the sutler's store. In fact, if he had money, he could buy a great many things, from clothing to writing material and stamps to newspapers and magazines. Then, as now, with money one could be relatively comfortable, even in prison. For most of the Confederates, though, getting the money would be the problem.

Federal greenbacks were the only money recognized by the Union troops, but they were not allowed inside the prison compound. When a prisoner arrived, any U. S. currency he had was taken and a credit was given him on an account at the sutler's store. Likewise, any money he received from family or friends during his stay was handled the same way—unless, of course, it was simply diverted by the Yankees into their own pockets. For a time, the sutler printed and issued his own notes based on a prisoner's credit balance, and these were used as money among the captives.[82]

Confederate money, considered worthless paper by the Yankees, also circulated among the prisoners and was legal tender among the loyal officers, who still hoped to some day be able to take it back to a free Southern Confederacy. Meanwhile, inside the "Bull Pen," as the prison compound was called, there was no shortage of ways to spend it. At most prisons of any size—North or South—the inmate population quickly established their own society within the walls, and with nothing but time on their hands, many inmates soon set up their own little enterprises.

Inside the compound at Johnson's Island, one could hire his laundry done, have his hair cut or his teeth filled, buy homemade pies, and even have his likeness drawn. Tailors made and repaired clothes, cobblers mended shoes, carpenters made chairs, stools, and desks, and amateur

---

82 Ibid., 17.

*Johnson's Island Sutler's Certificate, circa 1863.*
*Courtesy of the Rutherford B. Hayes Presidential Library, Fremont, OH.*

artisans made buttons and jewelry out of whatever materials came to hand. Talented and educated inmates offered instruction in music, foreign languages, and even military tactics to the less enlightened. Chess and debating clubs flourished, and Bible classes met daily.

Finally, the Confederate money was welcome in the most common recreation of all—gambling. Games of chance of all descriptions went on day and night. Many of the prisoners also speculated in the currency, buying it up with their sutler certificates on the belief that they would be exchanged soon and would have a chance to use it back home. That, of course, was a gamble in itself, so the exchange rate of the Confederate dollar versus the Federal greenback fluctuated with the latest rumor. By the time Burton arrived, in August 1863, the rate had settled at about twenty to one, naturally in favor of the greenback.[83]

*Author's note: Most of what we know about the day-to-day life inside Johnson's Island prison during the time Burton Warfield was there comes from the diaries of other prisoners, including one written by Capt. Robert W. Bingham, Company "G," Forty-Fourth North Carolina Infantry. Captain Bingham's diary is of special interest here since he arrived at Johnson's Island three weeks before Burton Warfield and was there for all but two months of Burton's stay. Not only were they there at the same time, but for at least three months, through the coldest part of the winter, they were in the same building, Block 8. Some of Bingham's friends among the North Carolina prisoners, mentioned by name in his diary, were actually Burton's mess mates. While only three of Burton's letter, and two of Anna's survive from*

---

83 Long, "Johnson Island Prison," 6ff and Robert W. Bingham, the Civil War Diary of Robert W. Bingham, Captain, Company "G," Forty-Fourth North Carolina Infantry Regiment (Local History File, Rutherford B. Hayes Presidential Center, Spiegel Grove, Fremont, Ohio).

*this period, Captain Bingham, who literally lived alongside Burton for those long months, wrote in his diary almost every day. Thanks to him, we know about Burton's life at Johnson's Island in great detail—what the weather was like on a given day, what the latest rumors were, what the food was like, and a hundred more details of camp life.*[84]

When it received its first prisoners in April 1862, Johnson's Island was commanded by a former mayor of Sandusky, William S. Pierson. He evidently had good political connections, but no military training. His guards consisted of four companies, about four hundred men, recruited locally and called the "Hoffman Battalion" after Colonel Hoffman who had built the prison. Pierson, who was commissioned a major and later promoted to lieutenant colonel, and commanded the prison for almost two years, was universally disliked by the southern inmates. He was considered petty and vindictive, and many of his regulations seemed designed for no other purpose than to harass the prisoners under his charge. Likewise, most of the men in his battalion of guards were scorned by the Confederate combat veterans as never having heard a shot fired in anger or seen a drop of blood shed in battle.[85]

---

84 Diary of Robert W. Bingham.
85 Long, "Johnson's Island Prison," 13ff.

## CHAPTER NINETEEN
## *"Fresh Fish!"*

August 11, 1863 was a windy day on Sandusky Bay, which made for a choppy passage for the *Island Queen* across the three miles to the military prison. Before long, though, the steamer was tied to the dock, and Burton Warfield and the others with him were marched across the parade ground to the main (western) gate of the stockade. Here they were checked in, assigned to a barracks or "block," as the buildings were called, and finally ushered into the compound.

As Burton stood just inside the main gate, he would have been looking east across the "Bull Pen," an area of about sixteen acres which was the prisoners' home. The whole compound was enclosed by a stockade fence about fifteen feet high with a walkway on the outside about four feet below the top, where sentries patrolled at all times.

On either side of the prison yard stood the blocks—six on each side. On the right were the odd-numbered blocks, with Block 1 being closest to the gate, and reserved for those prisoners who received special favors from the prison administration or who had taken the oath of allegiance, known as "Galvanized Yankees" by the prisoners. On the left were the even-numbered blocks, with Block 6 serving as the hospital. At the far end, in the center of the two lines, was Block 13. About thirty feet in from the fence, a line of stakes marked the "Dead Line." Just as the name implies, any prisoner approaching the fence nearer than the stakes

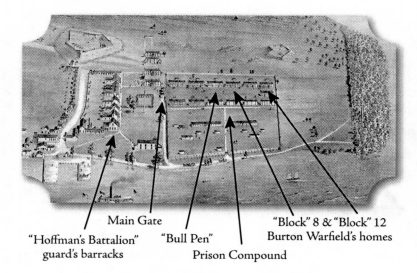

Main Gate

"Hoffman's Battalion"          "Bull Pen"          "Block" 8 & "Block" 12
guard's barracks                                   Burton Warfield's homes

                              Prison Compound

*Johnson's Island Prison. Sandusky, OH.*
*Image courtesy of KJA Consulting, Orlando, FL.*

*Dr. David R. Bush, Professor of Archaeology, Heidelburg College,*
*at excavation site near Block 4, Johnson's Island.*
*Photo from author's collection.*

without permission could be immediately shot. Finally, the stockade was surrounded on three sides by a ditch, to discourage tunnelers.

Upon entering the "Bull Pen," the first thing that would have hit Burton, a new arrival fresh from a pleasant voyage across the bay, was the smell. It didn't seem to bother the veterans, and before long, he would have been used to it, too, but that first encounter literally took one's breath away. There were several sources—uncollected garbage and personal hygiene issues, for instance—but overwhelming them all was the odor from the "sinks." Behind each block was a sink, an outhouse or privy. Unfortunately, underneath the thin layer of soil, the island sat on solid limestone, which meant the sinks couldn't drain as they should. New ones had to be dug frequently because the old ones were constantly overflowing, giving the whole compound its characteristic aroma. When Burton arrived, this process had already been going on for sixteen months.[86]

On the south side of the compound, behind the odd-numbered blocks and their associated sinks, was a large open area which the prisoners used for organized activities, the most popular being a new Yankee game called Base Ball, two separate words in 1863. The game was already being played in the Northeast at the beginning of the war, but it was in the prison camps that the Southerners learned it and then took it back home with them. Although the new game provided physical exercise, it also soon became, just like college and professional sports today, serious competition. Eventually, two rival clubs formed at Johnson's Island: the Southern Club, made up of junior officers, and the Confederate Club, made up of field grade officers, majors and above. The big championship

---

86 Ibid., 8.

game was played about four months after Burton was transferred, with the favorite, the Southern Club, coming from behind to win, nineteen to eleven. In what was certainly an understatement, one prisoner who was present noted in his diary that "Among sporting characters, a considerable amount of money changed hands."[87]

"Fresh Fish!" was the cry that Burton and the other new arrivals heard as they stepped into this small town of about 2,300 souls. That term was used by Confederate prisoners throughout the Union prison system to denote "New Guys," and it had both positive and negative connotations. On the one hand, here were new faces who had to be accommodated into the already strained facilities, but also, here were comrades who might be from old units or hometowns, might have common friends or relatives, and, most importantly, might have fresh news about the war. Real news from the outside was a precious commodity, and within minutes, or certainly within hours, they would all be picked clean for new information.

The first order of business for the new arrivals was to get settled in their accommodations. Burton was assigned to Block 12, the farthest building down on the left, or north side. These two-story buildings were anywhere from 117 to 130 feet long and twenty-four to thirty feet wide. A few were divided into small rooms, holding eight to ten men each, but most of them were divided into six large rooms holding as many as forty. The ones with the smaller rooms held about 150 prisoners, while the others held as many as 250 men.[88] Burton would have been assigned to a room, and within that room, to a bunk about three feet wide and six

---

87 Ibid., 20.

88 Charles E. Frohman, *Rebels on Lake Erie* (Columbus, OH: Ohio Historical Society, 1965), 4-5.

feet long, which he would have shared with another man. The bunks ran along the walls and were stacked three high.

The men in each block were divided into two groups, and each group, called a "Mess," chose representatives to deal with the prison officials in matters concerning food and mail, the two most vital subjects in the prisoners' world.[89] For food, each Mess was issued bread every day, and other rations every second day—beans, rice, hominy, beef, dried fish, coffee, and sugar. These were received by the Mess representative, and it was then up to each Mess to prepare the food as they saw fit, using one of two cook stoves in their block. Within each Mess, duty rosters were posted for "KP," as well as for the many other necessary housekeeping jobs, and everyone took his turn. Every large Mess further broke down into small groups of a few men each—friends or other officers from the same unit—and they augmented their rations with fresh fruits and vegetables and other things from the sutler's store or parcels from home, as their resources permitted.

Water for drinking or washing had to be carried in from the outside. What were generously called wells—actually just crude holes in the ground—were dug around the compound, but, since it was only eight feet down to the limestone, the water had a heavy mineral content and was never enough to supply over two thousand men in any case. To make up the shortfall, two pumps were set up on the south side of the compound, out past the Base Ball field, with pipes running down into Lake Erie. For most of the year, these provided better water and also exercise for the prisoners who worked them, but in the winter, they froze. When that happened, small groups of prisoners were allowed

---

89 In Block 12, Burton belonged to Mess 2.

out on the ice to cut holes and draw water from the lake.[90]

Food and water could keep body and soul together, but mail was quite often a prisoner's psychological lifeblood. Like the rations representative, each Mess also appointed a postmaster who handled the mail for the group. This officer committed to memory the names of all his men—normally 125 to 140 names—so that the mail could be handled promptly and no one was overlooked or his mail misplaced.[91] This was a post of great responsibility since few things could arouse a prisoner's passions quicker than interference with his mail. Unfortunately, the prisoners' mail was a literal gold mine for the Federal troops, as well.

All outgoing mail was reviewed by prison officials, and the stated policy was one page only. As we shall see, there were ways around that rule, but it was the incoming mail that held the most opportunities for mischief. All letters and parcels had to be opened prior to letting anything inside the compound, to guard against any contraband. The Confederates maintained, however, that much of what was confiscated, was simply stolen. Family members and friends from all over the North and South responded to the prisoners' requests for money by sending greenbacks to them in the mail—how else could they do it? All these letters were, naturally, opened by prison staff. It requires no stretch of the imagination to guess what happened. Writing after the war, the Confederate officer who served, for a time, as postmaster for Burton's Mess at Johnson's Island, explained it this way: "Everyone who thinks knows the fate of currency mailed in a letter plainly addressed, as the war regulations require, to a prisoner of war in a federal prison, where

---

90 Diary of Robert W. Bingham.
91 John Orr, Lt. Sixth Louisiana, "Prison Experiences," *Confederate Veteran*, Vol. XIX, No. 11, November, 1911, 532-533.

it has to be opened and examined by their enemies before delivery to the prisoners. Thousands of letters, and their contents, about which they were advised in various ways, never reached the prisoners, and many more thousands that were mailed never were delivered to them. Opening and examining the contents of letters for rebel prisoners in the office of a federal prison during the civil war was surely a fat job."[92]

In spite of the obstacles, mail did get through. Letters from home were precious, but parcels containing food, clothing, and other vital supplies were worth their weight in gold. As valuable as these packages were, the overwhelming number of men who received them shared their contents instead of hoarding them. Part of the food received might go to other members of the prisoner's small mess group, or a sick or wounded friend whose recovery was being hampered by the basic prison diet. If one was lucky enough to receive some new clothes from friends or family, his old ones would go to others who had no one on the outside to support them. If one received greenbacks to go in his sutler's account, he would probably loan some to a friend whose account was almost empty. Of course, not everyone was so noble, but a surprising percentage actually were.[93]

---

92 Ibid.
93 Ibid. Captain Bingham's diary contains dozens of examples of this kind of practice, by himself and many others that he knew.

## Chapter Twenty
### *Life in the Bull Pen*

When Burton Warfield walked into the compound at Johnson's Island on that August day in 1863, he saw many things which would become part of his day-to-day existence, in one form or another, in one prison or another, for the next twenty-two months. On the outside stairs at the end of one of the blocks, he might have seen a man standing a few steps above a crowd, reading aloud from a newspaper he had just received in the mail. In the shade of another building, there might have been a French class going on or a Bible discussion group. Inside, there might have been card games in one corner and someone making or engraving jewelry in another.

On this, his first day, he might also have been introduced to an activity he would come to know well, and it centered around an iron kettle full of boiling water, set over a fire. At first glance, the men gathered around it might look as though they were cooking a large stew, but, in fact, the steaming water was full of clothes. Boiling clothes, especially underwear, or "drawers," as they were called, was one of the few effective ways the prisoners had of combating one of their worst enemies: the common bloodsucking louse. Even boiling clothes, though, was only a temporary reprieve. Lice were so pervasive in the buildings and in the grass of the compound that it was only a matter of time before the infestation would be back. In any case, even a short period of relief was usually considered worth the effort.[94]

Other forms of wildlife in addition to the louse also prospered on the island. One in particular flourished amid the refuse and trash that a human community of several thousand inevitably generated. One prisoner, who arrived about six weeks after Burton, described his first night in Block 5 this way: "My first night in prison was disturbed by a grand drill of wharf rats. My bed was on the floor. The rats formed at the far end of the building and rushed to the other, then wheeled and returned, and the way their tails flopped on the floor at their wheeling has clung to my memory to this day. The rats ran over me roughshod, as I occupied part of their former drill ground."[95]

It's uncertain whether, by the end of August, Anna had received any word as to the place of Burton's imprisonment, but she did receive a letter from her younger brother. His name was Samuel Alonzo Worley, referred to as "Lonny" by Burton in some of his letters. Lonny Worley was two years younger than Anna, and was a private in Company "A," First Tennessee Cavalry, where Burton had been the first lieutenant. After Burton's capture, this unit had followed the Confederate army south to Chattanooga and then been sent northward toward Knoxville.

The mountains of East Tennessee were far different than the area around Maury County, as young Lonny was finding out. Union settlement was strong, and the Confederates were in danger, not only from Union troops, but also from the local populace. Although it was part of

---

94 Ibid. This activity of boiling clothes was, in fact, exactly what Captain Bingham was doing on the day that Burton entered the compound at Johnson's Island, as recorded in his diary entry for August 11.

95 J. J. Richardson of Paris, Texas. Given in an address to the United Confederate Veterans Camp #70. December 17, 1905. Copy from the R.B. Hayes Presidential Library, Fremont, Ohio.

his home state, Lonny Worley, as he wrote to his sister back home, was not impressed with the land or the people.

—⟋⟍—

*August 27, 1863*

*Dear Sister*

*I avail myself of the present opportunity to write you a few lines to let you know where we are. I suppose it has been some time since you heard from us. We have not had any hard service to do since we left middle Tenn. We have been stationed near Kingston[96] for some weeks past, until a few days ago. The Yanks crossed the mountains and we had to fall back across the river to prevent them from crossing. We moved down the river to this place last Tuesday. The enemy comes down to the river at different points most every day, but have not attempted to cross yet. An engagement may take place any day.*

*East Tennessee is a hard place. It is very poor country and a disagreeable one for Confederate soldiers to be in. Union men are as plentiful here as they are in Yankdom. It is dangerous for one man to go out alone by himself.*

*We are all very sorry Burt was captured, and more so because they do not exchange now. I hope an exchange may take place before long, so he may be released from prison and returned to his command.*

*Winter is fast coming on, and I fear, so the most of us will suffer very much, for we were hurried off from home so unexpectedly that we did not bring our overcoats nor blankets, nor scarcely anything else with us, and I fear we will not be able to get them.*

*We have heard from Maury County two or three times since the Yankees came in there but cannot hear from home. I am more than anxious to*

---

96 On the Tennessee River, south of Oak Ridge, Tennessee.

hear what they did to Pa.[97] Col. Ross arrived here yesterday and brought us news from your neighborhood. We do not expect to get back home anymore until peace is made, and I fear that will be a long time yet. We have been fairing very well here for ourselves and forage for our horses, but this country cannot supply us long. Everything is at a very unreasonable price. A private cannot buy things that he is almost compelled to have. Brown jeans is worth ten dollars a yard, and my pants are worn out now.

We are enjoying good health, and I hope these lines will find you in the same fix. We will send a pace of letters to your place. Send them down to our country the first chance.

Give my respects to Grandma, and to all inquiring friends.

May the blessing of heaven be with you all now and forever. Write every chance you have.

S.A. Worley

—⁘—

Ten days after Lonny Worley penned his lines to Anna from East Tennessee, Burton wrote his first letter as a prisoner that actually made it home, almost eight weeks after his capture. So far, he had received no reply to any of his earlier efforts. Whether this was his first letter from Johnson's Island is unknown, but letters required paper and pencil and envelopes and Yankee stamps, all of which required Yankee greenbacks, which Burton may not have had until now.

—⁘—

---

97 "Pa" refers to Lonny and Anna's father, Steven A. Worley, who was not in the Confederate army, but who, according to a later letter by Burton, was taken and held by the Federals for some time when they came into Maury County. See Burton's letter dated October 15, 1863.

*Samuel Alonzo Worley. Original oil circa 1890,
painted by his daughter Susan from Civil War tin-type.
Courtesy of Steven Worley (Samuel's great-grandson).*

*Johnson's Island near Sandusky, Ohio*

*Sept. 6th 1863*

*My Dear Anna,*

It is a pleasant task and a happy privalidge to write to you and at the same time I know not whether my letters reach you. I have been informed from a verry reliable source that the federals occupy Columbia, and have established a post there, and consequently they have regular mails. That being the case I can't see why you should not get my letters promptly. Bro. Harlan is at Columbia frequently. You will please get him to attend to your mail matter. My health is verry good. I still have a slight cough. This is quite a pleasant place for this season of the year, but I fear we will suffer here this winter if we are so unfortunate as to have to stay here. I don't see any prospect at this time of getting away soon. The Officers in command here are gentlemen and treat us verry well. We have no grounds for complaint.[98] Kaeiser was not well when I was at home. I am very anxious to hear from him and all the rest of you. We have preaching here three or four times a week, lectures, debating societies, Bible classes. I belong to a bible class. We have a concert once or twice a week which to some is quite entertaining. Send me D. M. Harris address if you have it. I have forgotten it. You will excuse my short letters. One page is all we are allowed to write.[99] Give my love to all

---

98 Every Confederate prisoner wrote home with the full knowledge that his letter would be read by those in charge of his prison. For that reason, and also to spare the family back home further anxiety, many comments about their captors are positive in prisoners' letters. Comments in private diaries and those made after the war are often quite different.

99 This restriction on the length of letters was in place at the time Burton wrote this letter. This seems to have been imposed mainly because of the workload on the Union personnel who were required to review all letters, and not as a punishment for the prisoners. Within a month or so, an arrangement would be worked out to permit longer letters.

*Yours truly*
*Burton Warfield*

—◊◊◊—

The day Burton wrote this letter, September 6, 1863, was a Sunday, which may explain his mention of belonging to a Bible class. As strange as it may seem to us today, among these hardened, veteran, combat soldiers, religious services and activities were very important parts of their prison life. Many had been devout churchmen before the war—and almost all of them were certain that God favored their cause—and many others, who had perhaps not been paragons of virtue before, began to see religion in a more favorable light, given their present circumstances.

On this same Sunday, Capt. Robert W. Bingham, Forty-Fourth North Carolina Infantry, wrote in his diary some of his thoughts about the religious activity at Johnson's Island, as follows.

*6 Sep. [1863] Sunday*
  *There are 5 or 6 chaplains here & some preaching officers—2 Cols., one Capt. All of them are inferior men but one, Col. Lewis of Arkansas, who is a most pleasing speaker & a man of ability. They preach twice Sunday & have lectures during the week & bible classes & seem to be in earnest. They always have good audiences. I heard a sermon this morning ... but Sunday is a painful day here—no calm, no holy quiet. There is, perhaps a little less gambling, but the same novel reading and perpetual noise. How I long for a quiet Sabbath at home with you, my darling.[100]*

---

100 Captain Bingham states at the beginning of his diary that it is intended to be read only by his wife, so many of his thoughts and observations are directed to her. One hundred and ten years later, Captain Bingham's grandson allowed the diary to be made available to researchers.

Out of necessity, religious life inside the walls of a Yankee prison took on a different form than many of the men were accustomed to back home. In their own communities, the different churches maintained their own buildings and fellowships, but now everyone was thrown together, and they soon realized that some adjustments had to be made. Preaching—public speaking—was done by many different men. Some were army chaplains or other ordained clergymen, but others were not, and a speaker's popularity seemed to depend more on ability than ecclesiastical position. The Bible classes also tended to be more lively, having members from a wide variety of religious backgrounds. In several prisons, the inmates also formed Christian Associations, mainly to care for the sick and destitute among them.

The combination of many different denominations inside the prisons made for some unusual situations, and sometimes called for creative solutions to problems not normally faced in the little country churches back home. Another entry in Captain Bingham's diary details one such instance.

*6 Oct.* [1863] *Tues.*

*... I attended the prayer meeting. It was a very interesting meeting. There were 4 who expressed a wish to join the Ch.* [church], *one the Pres. Ch* [Presbyterian Church]—*but there is no Pres.* [Presbyterian] *clergyman here—rather strange—one the Epis.* [Episcopal]—*but the Epis. chaplain has had nothing to do with our meetings. Applicants will be admitted into the Church of Christ and the church forms settled later.*[101]

---

101 Diary of Robert W. Bingham, October 6, 1863.

While it's possible that Burton attended the Bible class mentioned in the above passage, or at least heard about it, the main thing weighing on his mind was concern about conditions back home. Even though he had written home several times since his capture, Burton had so far received nothing in return. Finally, on October 14, they called his name during mail call, and he opened a letter from his wife for the first time in three months. The next day, as he enjoyed the beautiful Indian Summer weather, Burton sat down and wrote his answer. This letter goes well beyond the one-page limit he had mentioned a month before and reflects a change in prison policy concerning the prisoners' mail. A week or so earlier, the policy had been changed to allow letters of any length, provided that the prisoner paid 2½ cents per page for the extra office work. I'm sure Burton considered it money well spent.[102]

—⁂—

*Johnson's Island near Sandusky Ohio*

*Oct 15 1863*

*My Dear Anna,*

*I received your letter yesterday and was delighted and gratified to hear from home and to know that you were all well. I have been quite uneasy and even distressed about you all. Kaeiser was unwell when I left home and I, unfortunately falling into the hands of the enemy, could not hear from home. I had not heard one word from you until I recd your letter. I am truly glad to hear from you. You say Kaeiser is well and harty now. Tell him to be a good boy and learn to read [and] do what his Ma tells him. He will be five years old now in a few days. If I can I will bring him a pretty when I come home. How I would like to hear Minnie prattle.[103]*

---

102 Ibid.

103 Burton's daughter, Mary Burton "Minnie" Warfield, just turned two years old.

*I don't think she will forget me. You did not state whether you had received more than one letter from me. I have written several. Have you heard anything from Dick and Lonny lately. I am getting along here verry well now. I hope we will not remain here much longer. There is some prospect of an exchange of prisners soon. I hope to get away from here before winter sets in. It may be that we will have to remain here all the winter. If so I am not well prepared for a winter campaign this far north in the way of clothing. I think the last letter I wrote you was directed to Nashville in the care of Mr. Brantley. You did not state whether you received that one, or one of those sent directly to Columbia. Your letter was mailed at Nashville. I am a little puzzled to know how to direct a letter in order for you to get it. I get the "American Christian Review" every week. It pursues the same straite forward unequvicating course. Contains much religious instruction. I wrote for it. It is sent to me without money and without price. We have quite a jolly crowd here. All kinds of amusements from a Thespian society,[104] to ball and marble playing, and then again religious meetings, preaching, prair meetings and bible classes, debating societies and almost anything else you could think of. So many men confined here together who have been accustomed to mental and physical exercise must have something to employ the mind. We get the daily papers, and monthly periodicals— Harpers, Godeys, Waverly, etc. Yet amid all these the greater portion of time is occupied mentally in day dreams and nocumal visions of loved ones at home. We lie down to rest at night to visit perhaps the beautiful and magic world of dreamland, which mocks us with its unattainable witcheries. We rise in the morning to behold the beaming rays of the sun as he rises as it were from the lake with its sparkling beauty. Sometimes as*

---

104 Burton may have seen a production by this society, held the week before. There would also be another one eleven days later.

# REBEL THESPIANS!

| | |
|---|---|
| Acting and Stage Manager, | Maj. GEO. McKNIGHT. |
| Treasurer, | Lt. Col. J. C. HUMPHREYS. |
| Prompter, | Capt. J. R. FELLOWS. |
| Scenic Artist, | Maj. SMITH. |

The management in the highest possible spirits, take great pleasure in stating that, at an enormous expense, a selection of the very finest dramatic talent known in the OLD and the NEW WORLDS has been made for the special delectation of the reinforcements strategically sent to Johnson's Island by "Uncle Jeff." Every effort will be made by the management to astonish the natives in a most delightful manner. It is with feelings of pride that we point to the following

## BRILLIANT ARRAY OF TALENT!

COL. BROWN, of Georgia,
MAJ. McKNIGHT, of Louisiana,
CAPT. CUSSONS, of Alabama.
CAPT. FELLOWS, of Arkansas.
CAPT. WASHINGTON, of North Carolina.
CAPT. YOUNGBLOOD, of Tennessee.
CAPT. McLOCHLAN, of Kentucky.
MAJ. COOK, of Mississippi.
LIEUT. HOUSTON, of Virginia.
LIEUT. PEELER, of Florida.

### TOGETHER WITH

MISSES BROWN!
LAMAR!
COFFIN!
CANTRELL! and
STEWART!
AND A SUPERB CORPS DE BALLET !!!

## Wednesday Evening, Oct. 7, 1863

THE STANDARD COMEDY OF

# THE TOODLES!

| | |
|---|---|
| FARMER ACORN, | Capt. J. McLochlan. |
| GEO. ACORN, | Lieut. T. D. Houston. |
| TIMOTHY TOODLES, | Capt. J. W. Youngblood. |
| FARMER FENTON, | Maj. Cook. |
| CHARLES FENTON, | Maj. Bate. |
| LAWYER GLIB, | Lieut. Dismukes. |
| 1st FARMER, | Capt. Washington. |
| 2nd FARMER, | Lieut. Lauchlin. |
| 3rd FARMER, | Lieut. Long. |
| LANDLORD, | Taylor. |
| MARY ACORN, | Miss (Maj.) Stewart. |
| TABITHA TOODLES, | Miss (Col.) Jack Brown. |

SONG, · · · · · Capt. E. F. Lamar.

TO CONCLUDE WITH THE GREAT FARCE OF

# SLASHER & CRASHER!

| | |
|---|---|
| SLASHER, | Maj. Geo. McKnight. |
| CRASHER, | Capt. J. R. Fellows. |
| BLOWHARD, | Capt. J. W. Youngblood. |
| CAPT. BROWN, | Lieut. A. J. Peeler. |
| ROSA, | Miss (Maj.) Stewart. |
| DINAH BLOWHARD, | Lieut. Dismukes. |

In consequence of the immense expense attending the representation, the FREE LIST is ENTIRELY SUSPENDED!

An Orchestra, expressly provided, at an immense expense of Sutler's Checks, has arrived from Europe and other seaboard towns, and will entertain the appreciative audience with selections from the finest music ever heard on this or any other planet.

The Sentinels on the outer walls have been specially engaged to preserve order and decorum.

Little boys will not be allowed to eat pea nuts in the pit, nor throw orange peel from the gallery during the more affecting parts of the play. In order to carry out this arrangement more effectually, a special order will be issued, forbidding Joe Reynolds selling any of those articles to the little boys.

### PRICES OF ADMISSION.

| | |
|---|---|
| Dress Circle, | Twenty-five Cents. |
| Parquette, | Two Bits. |
| Pit, | Two Dimes and a half. |
| Gallery | Two Shillings. |
| Private Boxes, | Quarter of a Dollar. |
| Reserved Seats, to be had only on Tuesday morning after 10 o'clock, | Fifty Cents. |

---

# ISLAND MINSTRELS!

| | |
|---|---|
| Manager and Proprietor, | Mr. CHAS. L. STOUT. |
| Acting Stage Manager, | Mr. E. H. WALTER. |
| Musical Director, | Mr. W. H. HARRISS. |
| Treasurer, | Mr. J. C. WARD. |

The Manager having had forty years experience in his peculiar line of business, is proud to announce to the friends of the *Institution* and citizens of Johnson's Island, that after unparalleled exertions he has succeeded in procuring the first order of talent from Fort Delaware, Alton, Camp Chase, and the Penitentiarys of Columbus Ohio, and Alleghany City, Pa. He is now prepared to present to the public the greatest array of talent ever before witnessed in the United States. He has succeeded in procuring for one night only, the services of the

### FOR THE BENEFIT OF

# CHARLIE STOUT!

BILLY BOYD has volunteered his services for this occasion.

ALSO, THE FOLLOWING STARS:

MR. D. L. DUNHAM, the inimitable Bones,
MR. T. F. MITCHEL, the renowned Guitarist,
MR. J. C. WARD, the exquisite Flutist,
MR. WM. H. HARRISS, the modern Paganini,
MR. Ole Bull LIVINGSTONE,
MR. Paul Julien HANRAHAN,
MR. Joe Sweeney CRONIN,
MR. Triangular DECKER,
MR. CHARLES L. STOUT.

Feeling that he would not be able to do justice to his own merits, respectfully invites the Public to come and see what he can do with the Tamborine.

## Monday Afternoon, October 26th, 1863.

# PROGRAMME.

## PART FIRST.

| | |
|---|---|
| OPENING OVERTURE | Full Band. |
| "   CHORUS, | " |
| A LITTLE MORE CIDER, | Dunham. |
| TILDA HORN, | Ward. |
| YELLOW ROSE OF TEXAS, | Mitchell. |
| KATIE DEAR, | Livingstone. |
| VIRGINIA, | Walter. |
| SILVER SHINING MOON, | Stout. |
| CLAP YOUR HANDS FOR DIXIE, | Company. |

## PART SECOND.

| | |
|---|---|
| THE OFFICERS FUNERAL, (Trio,) | Harriss, Dunham & Mitchell. |
| PICAYUNE BUTLER IS COMING, | Company. |
| OUR GLORIOUS CONSTITUTION, (Lecture,) | Stout. |

Concluding with the

# CHECK APRON BALL!

| | |
|---|---|
| DINAH BLOSSOM, | Miss F. Mette. |
| BOB RIDLEY, | Boyd. |
| CHARLES AGUSTUS, | Dunham. |

## ADMISSION 25 CENTS.

| | |
|---|---|
| Reserved Seats, | 50 Cents. |
| Private Boxes, | $5.00. |
| Children, | 12½ Cts. |
| Niggers, | Free. |

*Flyers for shows produced by the prisoners at Johnson's Island during Burton Warfield's stay. Courtesy of Ruthorford B. Hayes Presidential Library, Fremont, OH.*

calm and placid as the bosom of the sleeping infant, not a breeze disturbs its smooth and limpid surface, then again foaming and surging in boisterous fury as if in its rage it would submerge our island home. The beautiful forest which adorns this island has put on its brown and somber appearance, much like our November the latter part. Just at this time the weather is quite pleasant. There is more than two thousand prisners here at this time, most of them officers. We are treated verry kindly. I was sorry to learn that your Pa is a prisner taken away from his family and home just at the time when they require his protection most. You did not tell me whether he lost any of his stock or negros. What has become of my horse, Gray Bell. My fine mare went up when I did as a matter of corse. I had the mortification of seeing her appropriated by a black hearted Tennessean who was piloting the Federals through our country. Did you make anything to eat. What for crop did you raise this summer. What has become of Tom Brooks?[105] I suppose you have heard of the death of Captain Sparkman who was killed at Port Hudson.[106] He was a very gallant officer and died heroically in defence of his country. Has Col. Miller come home? He was parroled at Port Hudson and John Miller. I would be glad to hear from the boys. How is Brother White getting along? Give my regards to him and family. I saw Frances the day I was captured. She wanted to go home. Did she come home? Tell Amaziah Young to write to me. Remember me to Bro. Harlan and family, old Uncle Jesse Brim and all the neighbors. I am in good health and spirits. The election for Govner of Ohio has just come off. Borough, the republican candidate, is elected by a large majority over Valandigham,

---

105 Tom Brooks, Burton's brother-in-law (and nephew), married to Anna's older sister, Mary. See note 62.

106 Capt. James Sparkman of the Maury Light Artillery, who was possibly related to some of the Warfields' neighbors.

*democrat. Give my love to mother. I often think of her and I know she will remember me in her prairs. Kiss the little ones for me. Write to me as soon as you get this, give me all the news.*

*As ever yours,*

*Burton Warfield*

—⚊—

After three months as a prisoner, Burton had finally established contact with Anna again. It is reasonable to believe that several more letters passed between them during the remainder of Burton's time on Johnson's Island, but only two survive—one from Anna and one from Burton. From other sources, however, we know a lot about the conditions that the POWs on Johnson's Island endured during the next few months.

Burton had expressed to Anna his concern about his ability to wage a "winter campaign" that far north because of the state of his clothes, and his concerns were well founded. Family and friends from the South, as well as individuals and benevolent organizations in the North sent clothes as best they could. We can only hope that Burton was one of the fortunate ones that received a warm coat or blanket before the snow came.

## Chapter Twenty-One
### Winter on Lake Erie

A s October came to a close, the weather remained mild and prison life remained mostly routine, but a few unusual events served to break the boredom. A rumor had been running through the prison that some of the Southern officers were planning a general uprising to overpower the guards, take over the island, and then find some way across the lake to Canada. When this rumor reached the Yankees, they reacted with considerable alarm, going so far as to bring in a gunboat to anchor just off shore and fire off some charges of grape shot to impress the would-be escapees. All this was taken in stride by the prisoners, many of whom were amused that the "brave" Yankees considered them such dangerous characters.[107]

In the middle of all this excitement, the Yankees also executed a prisoner, but he wasn't a Southerner. From time to time, Johnson's Island and other Federal prison camps housed civilians and Northern deserters, as well as Confederates. In this case, the man's name was Ruben Stout. He had deserted from the Union army and then killed one of the men who came to arrest him. On October 23, 1863, he was marched outside the stockade and shot by a firing squad. The prisoners were told to stay

---

107 Diary of Robert W. Bingham, 84-86.

indoors, but some of them watched anyway. Even though he was a Yankee deserter, Stout's execution had a sobering effect on everyone.[108]

As November began, the weather turned colder, bringing the first snow flurries and thin films of ice on the standing water in the mornings. Rumors of an escape attempt continued to circulate, which caused the Union commander to bring in more troops and increase restrictions on the prisoners. Finally, on November 12, he issued an order that caused quite a stir. The sutler's store was to be shut down. Everyone had an opinion as to the cause: retaliation for the treatment of Union prisoners in Southern hands, suspicion that the sutler was part of the escape plans, or simply a scheme to sell all the sutler's goods before the prisoners were exchanged and sent south. Whatever the truth, there was a great run on the store as the inmates tried to use up their balance on the sutler's account while there were still goods available.[109] In the middle of all this, Burton decided to make a move.

When a prisoner came to Johnson's Island, he was assigned to a building, or block, and he was required to stand for roll call in front of his block every morning as a guard checked his roster. It was possible, however, for a prisoner to move from one block to another, provided there was space available, the other prisoners involved agreed, and the guards were informed so that his name could be transferred to the correct roll book. At this time, Burton was in Block 12, and if he moved without notifying the Yankees, he would be counted as absent in the next roll call for that block, and the punishment for that could be severe.

On November 14, about one hundred "fresh fish" from North

---

108 Long, "Johnson's Island Prison," 29.
109 Diary of Robert W. Bingham, Nov. 12, 1863.

Carolina and Louisiana units came into the Bull Pen and were assigned to Block 8, which was empty at the time. Burton and several other men in Block 12 decided to move in with them, since Block 8 was broken down into several small rooms. Instead of forty to fifty men to a large room in Block 12, here the smaller rooms held six to ten officers. Not only were the rooms easier to heat, but they offered some small amount of personal privacy and quiet, which was a rare thing in a camp with over two thousand men jammed into a few acres.

One of the other men who made the move to Block 8 with Burton was North Carolina Capt. Robert Bingham, author of the diary which has provided valuable information and has already been cited several times. For the next three months, Bingham would be Burton's neighbor in Block 8, and at least two of his friends, mentioned by name in his diary—Capt. B. F. White of the Sixth North Carolina and Lt. R. E. Mayo of the Forty-Fourth North Carolina—would be Burton's mess mates.[110]

As November passed into December, there were good days, as well as bad. Some days the government rations were adequate, and other days they were short. On cold days, the pumps froze and, unless they were allowed to go out to the lake, the prisoners had little water. On warmer days, it often rained, turning the fifteen-acre enclosure into what Bingham called "a hog pen" and polluting the holes in the ground, which the Yankees called wells. Even though they sat a few yards from Lake

---

110 Diary of Robert W. Bingham, November 14, 1863, and Orr, "Prison Experiences." In this article, Mr. Orr, who was one of the "fresh fish" who moved in on November 14 and was then elected Postmaster of Block 8 Mess Number One, submits, after forty-seven years, the list of 125 names he memorized as part of his postmaster duties. This list includes Burton Warfield and the two North Carolina officers mentioned above. JRK

Erie, getting adequate fresh water for drinking and washing was a constant problem for the prisoners. About this time, however, a small bit of good news arrived. Mr. Johnson, the owner of the island, was allowed to re-establish the sutler's store.[111]

Christmas Day, 1863, was bright and warm, and the men of Johnson's Island celebrated as best they could. Those who had received food packages from home, or who had friends willing to share, were able to enjoy a good Christmas dinner. For the rest, government rations would have to do. The mild weather continued for the rest of the week, a sort of Christmas present for all the Southern soldiers. Even this, though, was not without its drawbacks. The warmer temperatures brought the lice and other insects back into action, as well as mice, which were becoming a real nuisance and, as always, there was the constant mud. Then, on New Year's Eve, winter came for real.

As the sun went down on December 31, 1863, it was raining on Johnson's Island with the temperature about fifty degrees. By sunrise on New Year's Day, it was below zero. Even the local men serving as guards were shocked. As is often the case, however, where most see adversity, some see opportunity. Knowing that the bitter cold would freeze the lake, some men began work on a makeshift ladder. The next night, after "light's out," five men, led by Capt. John R. Winston of North Carolina, went over the wall. By then, the temperature was twenty below zero, and the guards were so busy trying to keep warm that nobody noticed. Most of their fellow prisoners were sure the five men would freeze to death. In fact, one of the men was later captured and lost several fingers to frostbite, but the other four not only survived the bitter cold, but eventually

---

111 Diary of Robert W. Bingham, December 13 and 17, 1863.

made it to Detroit and across the river into Canada.[112]

The weather moderated for a couple of weeks, but a heavy snowstorm came in on the nineteenth, setting the stage for one of the strangest battles of the war. The next day, hundreds of prisoners formed up into two brigades, complete with flags and uniforms and commanded by a senior officer, and charged each other in what one prisoner called a "magnificent snow fight." A few black eyes and bloody noses were the only casualties, and a good time was had by all.[113] Whether Burton was involved in the snowball battle is not known, but a few days later, he had a chance to speak his mind on a matter of Tennessee politics.

A local judge had published an open letter in a Nashville paper, urging the people of Tennessee to accept the terms of amnesty recently offered by President Lincoln and organize a state government loyal to the Union. When word of the letters reached Johnson's Island, a number of Tennessee officers formed a committee for the purpose of drafting a reply. The result was a wonderful bit of classic Victorian prose which, in spite of its flowery and lofty phrases, left little doubt where Tennessee's Confederate POWs stood on the matter. The following is the text of their response:

—ɯ—

*Johnson's Island, Jany 27, 1864*

*We, the undersigned, Confederate officers from the state of Tennessee, but now imprisoned within this bastille of Lincoln despotism, have recently had our attention called to a letter of the Hon. Edwin H. Ewing, addressed to friends in Nashville, and published in a sheet known as the*

---

112 Long, "Johnson's Island Prison," 28 and Diary of Robert W. Bingham, January 2, 1864.
113 Diary of Robert W. Bingham, January 20, 1864.

*Daily Press of that city, calling upon the people of the state to accept the terms of amnesty contained in a recent proclamation of Lincoln, and to organize the State Government.*

*Impotent as the voice of the chained captive may be, we cannot remain passive while a proposition so infamous and abhorrent to every man of spirit and honor is submitted to our suffering countrymen. Does not the blush of shame mantle your cheek, sir, when you propose to your fellow citizens, environed around about with all the energy of oppression, terms so disgraceful, so humiliating, so repugnant to every manly and noble sentiment of our nature? Why add insult to injury? Why not, with your worthy coadjutors, your Houstons, your Bryans, your Stokes and Campbells, establish your government and cram it down the throats of the people, without seeking to extort a seeming acquiescence and submission to a government which every true man in Tennessee hates with all the ardor of his noble soul?*

*...signed: Geo. W. Winchester, chairman*[114]

—◊◊—

Attached below the text were the names of two hundred Tennessee officers, including Burton Warfield, Alfred Osburne Pope Nicholson, who was captured with Burton at Columbia, and Tod Carter from Franklin, Tennessee, one of Burton's mess mates from Block 8.

---

114 Frank H. Smith, *History of Maury County Tennessee* (Columbia, TN: Maury County Historical Society, 1969), 80.

## Chapter Twenty-Two
### *False Hope*

As February began, one of the camp's most persistent rumors actually came true—not a mass escape, as the Yankees had been expecting, but the beginning of the transfer of men south and east to be exchanged, or so it was said. On the morning of February 9, men's names were called, all beginning with A, B, or C, and they were told to pack their things. By that evening, four hundred had been taken. Finally, the hope of being moved off what Burton would later call "that detestable island" had come true. Unfortunately for Burton, having a name beginning with "W," his turn wouldn't come for two more months. Meanwhile, a couple of days later, Burton's mess mate, Tod Carter, who was in the first group, took advantage of an open window and jumped off the train somewhere in Pennsylvania. Tod made his way back to his old unit, the Twentieth Tennessee Infantry, in time to be mortally wounded in the backyard of his own home during the Battle of Franklin, ten months later.

The day after the first group of men left Johnson's Island was Burton and Anna's sixth wedding anniversary, and he was having to spend it in a cold and muddy prison, five hundred miles from home. Back in Tennessee, Anna sat down to write him a letter on their special day, to let him know he was not forgotten. It seems only fitting that this is the first letter from Anna to survive. Somehow, Burton managed to hold on to this and several other of her letters over the next sixteen months, and bring them home.

While the weather in Maury County was much nicer and things on the farm seemed to be under control, other things going on at church and among the neighbors had Anna distressed. She was particularly upset by the behavior of two women, members of her church, whose husbands were also prisoners of war, but whose conduct Anna thought very unbecoming. There was also a problem with a military officer (probably Union), but apparently, it had been resolved. This letter is a subtle reminder that, for a Southern woman, life on the home front held its own problems and dangers. Finally, there was the simple wish that Burton would be able to come home and they could have a normal life.

—⁓—

*Stony Point*

*Feb the 10th 1864*

*Dear Burton*

*I told you in my last letter that I would write again in a few days. Having an opportunity to send a letter tomorrow I will write a few lines. We have been gardening today. The weather has been so pleasant we could not wait any longer. I recon you remember six years ago from today how very cold the weather was. Nearly all the farmers have commenced ploughing. The boys will be ready to commence next week. They are repairing the fences now. Seem to be doing very well.[115] The disease that raged so in our neighborhood has ceased but there is another disturbance now. There have been a few parties or dances rather in the neighborhood and some of our Bro and Sisters have been dancing. You will be surprised*

---

115 From this comment, we know that Anna had help on the farm. Whether the mention of "the boys" refers to slaves, hired men, or male relatives is never quite made clear.

*Martha and Nan White were the ladies that danced had just received letters from their husbands at Rock Is Ill.*[116] *Instead of praising of our heavenly Father for sparing their lives they have gone so far from their sense of duty. I think Christians ought to be more on their guard now than they ever were. We are commanded to shun all appearance of evil. Bro. White is very badly hurt about the way the members of the church are doing. We have meeting at Liberty now. Sister Blocker is going to move to Williamsport. I saw Bro. Young yesterday. He said he had written three letters to you and had not received a letter in return. If you received my letter I hope you will not be pesterd as bad when you read it as I was when I wrote it. Capt. Ourst [sic] did not understand me in my letter previously. I suppose I would have gone up and seen him but have not had an opportunity. I hope I will never get in another difficulty. The greatest pleasure that I have now is that I can hear from you. I pray the Lord may spare our lives that we may see each other again. We have lived together three years out of six. We are all well. I will close. Write soon.*

*As ever yours*

*Anna*

—◊—

Some more letters were written during the rest of February and March which do not survive, but finally, at the first of April, Burton was able to write Anna a letter that, while short, was filled with more optimism than he had felt in a long time.

—◊—

*Johnsons Island*

*April 4, 1864*

*My dear Anna*

---

116 Another Union prison camp

*I received your letter of the 27th today. I recd. one the 1st inst. which I answered on the 2nd. My health has improved much for the past 2 or 3 days. Our letters seem to go through when they do go at all, in a bunch. You got two from me in one week when you had not received one for three or four wks. previous, and I 2 in four days when I had not recd. one for two months before. I am glad Bro Beasley is coming to our neighborhood. You will have some preaching now. We have preaching here of all sorts and sizes. Several prisoners were baptized a Sunday or two ago—Easter Sunday I think. Eleven were buried in the blue waters of Erie amid the ice and snow. You say Tite Edwards is at home—going into the cotton business. He won't make enough to pay taxes.[117] Has he taken the oath or been paroled. Amos Seely has taken a French furlough.[118] Well "bully for him." We are getting along very well here and looking forward with buoyant hopes and expectations to the time when we will be exchanged. Tell Kaeiser to learn to read and be a good boy. I will write him a letter some of these days—He is all right!*

*Remember me to all*
*As ever yours,*
*Burton Warfield[119]*

—⚬⚬⚬—

On April 22, 1864, Burton's turn finally came, and he left Johnson's Island. His hope was that he would be exchanged, but that would probably mean going through Richmond, a city where he would be a stranger—just one among thousands of soldiers. To help Burton along, one of his fellow prisoners, who had connections in the Confederate

---

117 Edwards was a sergeant in Burton's unit.
118 Slang term for going AWOL—"taking French leave"
119 This letter (April 4, 1864) is present only in the *Historic Maury* collection.

capitol, provided him with a letter of introduction to a man of some prominence.

—⁓—

*Johnsons Island*
*April 22, 1864*
*Hon. James C McCullim*

*My Dear Sir, allow me to introduce to your favorable consideration Lt. Warfield who has been regularly in the Confederate service & is not acquainted with anyone in Richmond. Any favor you do him will be a favor to me & a good soldier.*

*Receive for yourself my best wishes with many hopes for our success. Believe me when I tell you I have a great desire for release and a return to my native state.*

*I have been faring well and will abide my time with patience.*
*Yours truly M. Galloway*
*Captain C.S.A.*[120]

—⁓—

As luck would have it, a letter from Anna arrived a few days after Burton's departure, but one of his friends answered it, and in this way, Anna found out about Burton's transfer.

—⁓—

---

120 Burton, unfortunately, had no chance to use this letter at the time it was written, since he was not exchanged or released for another fourteen months. The letter is almost certainly addressed to James McCallum, a prominent citizen of Giles County, Tennessee, and a Representative to the Second Confederate Congress. He would have been in Richmond at the time. The identity of "M Galloway, Captain, CSA" is still a mystery, although it is possible that he was Capt. M. G. Galloway, First Arkansas Mounted Rifles, who was wounded at Murfreesboro, Tennessee, on December 31, 1862. JRK

*Johnsons Island, Ohio*

*April 27th 1864*

*Mrs. Burton Warfield*

*Yours mailed 21st inst came to hand to day & in the absence of your husband, & by his request, I am given to write you a few lines informing you that he left us on the 22th inst., either an exchange or to point look out with the convaliscent of the prisoners of this prison.[121] He was doing very well the day he left nothing serious with him. He wrote to you the day before he left and requested me to mail it the following day, which I did. He promised to write to me as soon as practicable. As soon as I hear from him I will write you again. The health of the Maury County Boys are very good at presant. As I have nothing of particular interest I will close*

*If this meets with your approbation an answer would be very agreeable.*

*I am Respectfully,*

*Joseph Foster, Capt C.S.A.[122]*

—⁓—

Burton had finally gotten half of his fondest wish—he was free of Johnson's Island—but the other half—being exchanged back to Dixie— would continue to elude him.

---

121 Evidently, the prisoners selected for transfer were taken from those with significant health problems. Point Lookout, Maryland was the biggest Union prison camp and had a large medical facility. Both Captain Bingham, the diarist who left in the first group, and Burton, who arrived two months later, wrote their first entries or letters after arriving at Point Lookout from one of the wards at Hammond Military Hospital. JRK

122 This was Capt. Joseph M. Foster, Company "D," Cooper's Tennessee Cavalry, a unit raised near Burton's home in Maury County. The Union considered them little more than partisans and "bushwhackers," and the unit was broken up in early 1864 after the capture of their commander Major Cooper. Foster was captured in late 1863, and is listed, along with Burton, as part of the committee replying to Judge Ewing's letter on January 27, 1864. He is also listed as one of Burton's mess mates in Block 8. JRK

# Chapter Twenty-Three
## *Point Lookout*

*T*he three main Union prisons, which would be Burton Warfield's home for two years, all had one thing in common. Their primary security was water. Johnson's Island had been surrounded by Lake Erie, and Point Lookout was situated at the very tip of a peninsula in southern Maryland, bounded by the Potomac River and the Chesapeake Bay. The third one, still to come, would also be an island.

Like those before them, Burton's group traveled by train from Sandusky, Ohio, to Baltimore, where they boarded a boat for the trip down the Chesapeake Bay to Point Lookout. On April 26, four days after leaving Johnson's Island, Burton was admitted to Hammond General Hospital, Ward #2. The diagnosis of his illness was not very elegant or heroic, but was a complaint common to cavalrymen since the days of Alexander the Great—hemorrhoids.[123] All in all, though, Burton's situation had improved greatly. Back on Johnson's Island, to be sent to the hospital inside the compound was to put a sick man's life in even further jeopardy. The facilities at Hammond Hospital at Point Lookout, on the other hand, were clean and orderly, all the patients had iron cots, mattresses, and lamps, and the staff was competent and attentive.[124]

---

123 Warfield Official Records.
124 Diary of Robert W. Bingham, February 14, 1864 and following entries.

Things were definitely looking up. The change in Burton was evident in his next letter home, which he wrote five days after arriving.

—∞—

*Hammon General Hospital*

*Point Lookout May 1st 64*

*My dear Anna*

*When I wrote you last from Johnsons Island I informed you that I was about starting as I thought for Dixie to be exchanged but I was stoped here. I am truly glad to get away from that detestable island. This is quite a pleasant place, situated on the Chesapeake Bay in Maryland. My health has improved a great deal since I left the island. I am in the hospital here, a very nice place, everything neat and clean. Much better than the hospital at Johnsons Island. And then we have more latitude here. Can walk up and down the beach, pick up nice pebbles and shells etc. The attendants and the officers in charge here are very kind to us. I hope to be exchanged soon. You must write to me as soon as you learn where I am. Direct your letter to Point Lookout, Md., Hammon General Hospital Ward no. 2. I have met here a son of Elisha Worley who belongs to the Rebel Army. He was wounded at Gettisburg, Pa. last July. He has had his right leg amputated. He is well now and wants to get south. His name is Columbus. They call him Fayet. My love to all.*

*As ever yours*

*Burton Warfield*[125]

—∞—

Life in the wards of Hammond Hospital was quite an improvement over the mud and stink of the Bull Pen at Johnson's Island, but it was only for the sick or wounded. Burton got to enjoy it for three weeks, but

---

125 *Historic Maury*, Vol. 5, No. 1, 2-8 & No. 2, 27-31.

Hospital

Prison Camp

Hammond Military Hospital and prison camp at Point Lookout, MD circa 1864. Image courtesy of KJA Consulting, Orlando, FL.

on May 17, he was returned to the general population in the main prison camp. From the relative calm and cleanliness of the hospital ward, he stepped into the hustle and bustle of a huge tent city.

When Burton had arrived, during the last week in April, the prison population at Point Lookout was already almost three times what he had experienced at Johnson's Island—over 6,000 men. Before he was released from the hospital, however, events conspired to make even that number seem a distant memory. During the first week of May, General Grant, now personally commanding the Army of the Potomac, crossed the Rapidan River and forced General Lee to meet him in two weeks of carnage which became known as the Battles of the Wilderness and Spotsylvania Court House. These battles produced 50,000 casualties— killed, wounded, missing, and captured—18,000 of them Confederate. While Burton had been basking in the relative comfort of the hospital, new prisoners had been streaming in from Virginia, just across the bay. When he walked into the prison camp on May 17, it contained almost 12,000 men.[126]

Settling in and finding his place among such a multitude took a while, but five days later, Burton found time to write his next letter.

—⚬⚬⚬—

*Officer's Camp Point Lookout Md*
*May 22 1864*
*My Dear Anna*

*I again attempt to address you a few lines. I have written to you so often without hearing a word from you that I have almost come to the conclusion to quit writing for a while. But the hope that you receive my*

---

126 Edwin W. Beitzell, *Point Lookout Prison Camp for Confederates* (Leonardtown, MD: St. Mary's County Historical Society, 1972), 41.

*letters and that it is some consolation to you to hear from me, induces me to write often. My health has improved some since I came to this place. We have been removed from the hospital to the prison camp. We are in tents now. This is quite a pleasant place, and I think verry healthy. We have the privilege of bathing in the bay which is salt and I think verry condusive to health. I left word with my friends at the island to forward here any letters that should come there for me but I have not received any from that source yet. I am indeed verry anxious to hear from you and can't imagine why I do not get letters from home. Others here get letters regularly from Columbia. How are you getting along farming? What is the prospect for fruit this year? How is my little rebel getting along and my little Minnie? I trust you have not all forgotten me. I am in good spirits and thank God for his goodness and mercy towards [me] and hope I may soon regain my wanted health. I send you a specimen of sea weed or moss which I have prepared. I have several specimens I wish to take home with me. My love to mother and all my friends.*

*As ever yours*

*B. Warfield*

—⚊—

For once the Yankee mail service worked very well, and Burton's letter arrived back home in only nine days. Anna sat down the next day and wrote her answer. In it she included some of the local news Burton craved and gave an upbeat account of things on the farm. She seemed to sense that knowing his family members were faring well back home was very important to Burton's morale.

—⚊—

*Stoney Point*

*June the 2nd 1864*

*My Dearest Burton,*

I received your letter of the 22nd of May yesterday with much pleasure and satisfaction. It had been over two weeks since I heard from you. I supposed you had been exchanged and would not get to hear from you in a long time. I hope you will regain your health now as summer has come. I recon I will have to quit thinking about you getting home soon for it seems you are destined to remain in prison for some time yet, but I pray the Lord to be with you and keep you from harm where ever you may be. The boys are getting along very well farming. Do a great deal better than they did before Dan left. I sent to Columbia and got old Henry without any trouble. Dan had been trying to sell him but had not succeeded. We do not feel any loss by him being gone. He had not ploughed any this year. The boys do a great deal better without him.[127] Our wheat is very good, our garden better than it has been for three or four years. I went to an exhibition last night at Harlen's schoolhouse and carried Kaeiser. He was so amased he did not think about going to sleep. George Mathews has come by for my letter and I will have to close as he is in a great hurry. I will write again in a few days. We are all well. Don't you quit writting often because you do not get my letters. Write often for you have nothing else to do. Nothing more

Yours as ever

Anna

—⁂—

Anna Warfield was right about one thing. Burton probably didn't have much of anything better to do than write letters home. Just because prison life might be boring most of the time, however, didn't mean there weren't new and fascinating things to see. For men who had never ventured far from their landlocked homes, living on the seashore

---

127 "Dan" was possibly an overseer for "the boys," most likely slaves. "Old Henry" appeared to be a slave. Whatever Dan's position, he was gone, and everything seemed better for it.

was a new experience, and the opportunity to bathe in the salt waters of the Chesapeake Bay was something that Burton and many others enjoyed immensely. It was probably in the camp at Point Lookout that Burton also saw, for the first time, a phenomena that spoke volumes about the future—Black Union Army troops.

Surely there had been rumors about the Yankees raising such units, but the first time they actually appeared was a shock to the Southern men. Here is how one Confederate soldier recorded in his Point Lookout diary his first sight of "Negro" troops:

*Wednesday, February 24, 1864. Clear and pleasant. Had a shower of rain last night. The Yankees gave our division pants.* For the first time in my life I have seen a regt. of Negro troops in full uniforms and with arms.

*Thursday, February 25, 1864. Clear and pleasant.* Negro soldiers were put on post to guard us. Was there ever such a thing in civilized warfare?[128]

Capt. Robert Bingham from North Carolina, the officer whose diary told so much about life at Johnson's Island, was also at Point Lookout and also witnessed the arrival of the Black troops on February 24. Still faithfully writing in his diary every day, even after his move, here is how Captain Bingham recorded the events of the next day:

*25 Feb. '64 ... But we did have something this morning. There was a crowd at guard mounting—as tho' something was to pay—& pretty soon a relief of the 2nd N. C. Vols, colored, marched round and were posted & we are*

---

128 Beitzell, *Point Lookout*, 69. Quoted from the diary of Private Charles Warren Hutt, C. S. A.

*guarded by Negroes. What do you think of that? For my part I think a black Yankee less a scoundrel than a white one. It is intended doubtless as an insult & humiliation to us, but I think it humiliates the Yankees more than us. This is a fair example of the action of the Yankee brute...*[129]

Bingham's opinion that the Black troops had been brought in to humiliate the Southern soldiers was almost universally shared by the other Confederate prisoners, and was surely true, to some extent. There were, however, other reasons as well.

Even in the enlightened and presumably abolitionist North, there were grave misgivings about these new troops, especially among some of the Union army officers who would command them, as all the Black units had white officers. In many cases, the Black troops were assigned to work gangs or, as in the case of Point Lookout and several other prisons, to guard duty. This not only freed up what many commanders considered more reliable white troops for combat, but in the second instance, also provided an opportunity to add insult to the already considerable injury visited on the Confederate prisoners.

By the time Burton arrived, the Black troops had been on duty for two months, and had ceased to be much of a novelty to the oldtimers. They had, however, carried on the tradition of the white New Hampshire troops, who had gone before them, by regularly killing or maiming prisoners by accidental discharges of their rifles or, as most Confederates believed, simply shooting men with little or no provocation. One man was shot after taunting a white Union sergeant, and another was killed when a guard heard talking after lights out and fired into a tent. Sometimes there was an investigation and punishment of the guard involved.

---

129 Diary of Robert W. Bingham, February 25, 1864.

Sometimes not. Either way, it was small comfort to the victim.[130] There was a measure of what the Southerners considered "poetic justice," however. Several times the guards also killed themselves or another guard by the mishandling and accidental discharge of their own weapons.

When Burton arrived at the end of April, conditions at Point Lookout were a great improvement over his former home on Lake Erie, but by the end of May, things had taken a decided turn for the worse. The renewed fighting in nearby Virginia had doubled the prison's population in the last forty-five days, and by the end of June, it would reach almost fifteen thousand. The already strained facilities were simply being overwhelmed.

All this had its inevitable effects. In May, in spite of the prisoner build up, Point Lookout reported only twenty-four deaths with just under one thousand sick, but in June, the sick number jumped to 1,400 and the deaths quadruped. The main culprit, most agreed, was bad water. With the total number of personnel to be supported approaching twenty thousand, plus a large number of livestock, the amount of water required each day was immense, especially with summer coming on. One of the Union doctors finally had the courage to state the obvious. Point Lookout couldn't take any more men. On June 23, Surgeon J. H. Thompson wrote, "I protest against the reception of additional numbers of prisoners, there being now fully 14,000 within the camp and near 20,000 on the Point in all ... In addition to this there are the quartermaster's stables with, I suppose, 250 horses and mules ..." Thompson goes on to say that there was insufficient water of bad quality, which was the main cause of the increased numbers of sick and dead. At that time, ten men a day were dying.[131]

---

130 Beitzell, *Point Lookout*, 27ff.
131 Ibid., 40.

When Burton arrived at Point Lookout, it had been a welcome relief from Johnson's Island. Now, sixty days later, it had deteriorated to the same level or worse—the same eternal mud, worse water, and six times as many prisoners. The prison officials were aware of the situation, too, and were already working to relieve the pressure on their facilities. In this case, however, they were probably just shifting the problems from one place to another. On the same day that Union Surgeon Thompson wrote his note, quoted above, Burton and a number of other prisoners were loaded on a boat and sent off, not south to be exchanged, unfortunately, but north to another prison.

# CHAPTER TWENTY-FOUR
## *Fort Delaware*

*"I hope it will not prove to be any worse than Point Lookout got to be."*
*(Burton Warfield)*

On June 25, 1864, Burton Warfield stepped off the Union transport boat onto the low lying, boggy shore of Pea Patch Island, in the middle of the Delaware River. Several hundred yards in the distance he could see the wooden barracks, much like the ones on Johnson's Island, and as he got closer, he was greeted by the familiar aroma of a prison camp, a mixture of thick, moist air, mud, garbage, and the combined presence of nine thousand dirty, ragged, hungry souls. Dominating the scene was a huge stone fort, complete with what looked like a medieval moat and drawbridge.

Fort Delaware was built in the 1840s and 50s to protect the cities further up the river—Wilmington and Philadelphia—but now, its cannon guarded Confederate POWs. At the far end of the drawbridge was a sally port providing entry into the fortress, and it was here that prisoners could often be seen experiencing a common form of punishment—being hung by their thumbs. This would be Burton's home for the next three hundred fifty days.

The next day, a Sunday, Burton wrote to Anna with the news of his new situation.

—⁂—

*Fort Deleware, Del.*

*June 26 1864*

*My Dear Anna,*

My place of imprisonment has been changed again. I am now at Ft. Deleware on the deleware river near Deleware City 35 or 40 miles from Philadelphia. We arrived here yesterday, whether for the better or worse I can't say yet. I hope it will not prove to be any worse than Point Lookout got to be. Our fair is very bad here and does not at all agree with me.[132] I want you to see Bro. Young and tell him to send me some money, he is owing me and will probably be glad [to] furnish me some money in that way a small amount. It is quite essential that I should have some money here and if it is sent by express, which it must be if sent at all, I will be very apt to get it. I learn that they deliver money sent here to prisoners verry promptly. My money left at Johnsons Island has never been heard from. My health is tolerable good at this time. Write to me soon and often. My love to all.

As ever yours

Burton Warfield

*Address*

*Lt. Burton Warfield*

*Prisoner of War 33 Division*

*Ft. Deleware, Del*

—〰—

The true origins of Pea Patch Island are lost to history, but the predominate story involves a ship, which is said to have run aground on a shoal in the early 1700s. Its cargo—peas—then sprouted and flourished,

---

132 After only one day, Burton had already formed the same opinion of the food at Fort Delaware, which was shared by almost every prisoner who was there. JRK

trapping debris and eventually forming a low, marshy island. The island was first proposed as a site for fortifications in 1794 by Pierre Charles L'Enfant, the famous French engineer who had taken time off from designing the new Federal City, which would become Washington D. C., to survey the Delaware River coast for just such places. The title to the land had been argued over in court, and work on fortifications had been started and then abandoned over the years. Finally, in January 1861, after twenty-nine years of work and the stupendous cost of $1,300,300, in mid-nineteenth-century dollars, Capt. John Newton reported that even though some interior work remained to be done and less than half its planned compliment of 156 guns were mounted, Fort Delaware was ready for occupation.[133]

What the army and the government got for all its effort and money was the largest and most modern fortification in North America. Fully armed and staffed, Fort Delaware would have made any attempt by enemy ships to sail up the Delaware River to assault the cities of Wilmington and Philadelphia suicidal. That, at least, is what everyone believed. In its eighty-four-year history, no enemy ever tried. Instead, for the first four years of its life, it became the nation's most heavily fortified prison camp.

Fort Delaware's location had a lot to recommend it, from a security point of view. It was, after all, in the middle of a large river, with the shoreline at least a mile away on either side. As a long time home for thousands of people, however, (for a brief period during the Civil War, Fort Delaware was, on the basis of population, the largest city in the state) it had serious problems. For all its grand sounding military title, the island was essentially a seventy-five-acre mud flat, with an average

---

133 Dale Fetzer and Bruce Mowday, *Unlikely Allies: Fort Delaware's Prison Community in the Civil War* (Mechanicsburg, PA: Stackpole Books, 2000), 1, 20-30.

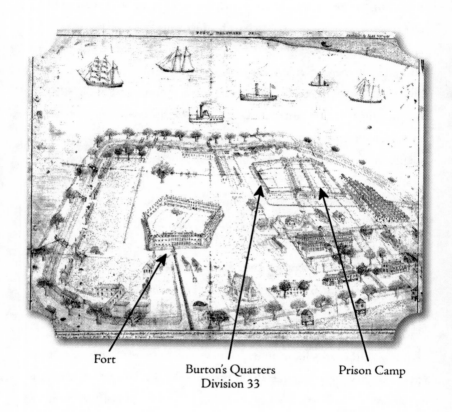

Fort         Burton's Quarters        Prison Camp
                  Division 33

*Sketch of Fort Delaware drawn by Max Neugas circa 1864.*
*Image courtesy of The Historical Society of Delaware.*

height above sea level of just over three feet. Being in the middle of a tidal river, this meant that at certain times, were it not for the military-built sea walls, parts of the island would literally be awash. Drinkable water was scarce and brackish, as opposed to river water which was everywhere.[134]

When Burton Warfield arrived at Fort Delaware, it had been in use as a prison camp for two years. Thousands of men had already passed through, and over nine thousand were currently in residence. During Burton's year there, the population would never fall below seven thousand. Although Burton had said, in his letter home, that he didn't know yet if this move was "for the better or the worse," we can be sure that, knowing Fort Delaware's fame, he feared the worse. A North Carolina prisoner said that by late 1863, Fort Delaware's reputation was such that news of being sent there would cause men's "faces to grow white and their hands to clench in fear."[135]

Simply put, the Fort Delaware that Burton Warfield found at the end of June 1864, was a hell hole. No question about it. Unfortunately, by this stage of the war, the same could be said for almost every other POW camp, North or South. The buildings, when there were buildings and not tents, were temporary or worse. Thousands of feet had turned the grounds into either dust or mud, depending on the weather. The food was bad, and the water was worse. The mail was slow, and the prospect of exchange was, for most, a distant dream.

By mid-1864, to be an inmate in *any* military prison camp, Union or Confederate, was a nightmare. To be fair, however, even though Fort Delaware had a reputation among the Confederate prisoners as a terrible

---

134 Ibid.
135 Speer, *Portals to Hell*, 143.

place—and it was—statistics studied after the war would show that it was much more survivable than other places like Elmira, New York, in the North, or Andersonville, Georgia, in the South.

This was Burton's third major prison camp, so he knew the drill: line up, be processed in, and find a place to live. The prison compound was several hundred yards northwest of the fort and covered about eight acres, divided into officer and enlisted compounds. This made it about half the size of the stockade area at Johnson's Island, but holding almost four times the number of men. The prisoners were housed in long barracks which had one continuous roof, but were divided up inside into rooms, or divisions. Each division was nineteen feet wide and sixty feet long, with bunks around the walls, three high, holding between four hundred and nine hundred men.[136]

From Burton's first letter from Fort Delaware, we know that he didn't like the food, which comes as no surprise. Nobody else liked it either. Part of the problem was the way it was served. Back at Johnson's Island, the prisoners got to do their own cooking, and so could, with a little imagination, improve on the plain government rations. At Point Lookout and at Fort Delaware, the prisoners were marched into a mess hall, where they found their rations on the table in front of them. It was either take it as it was or go hungry.

There were two meals a day. By the summer of 1864, the morning meal consisted of two hardtack crackers and a square inch of pickled meat. The evening meal was the same with the addition of a cup of bean soup. With the lack of vegetables, about 12 percent of the men had scurvy.[137]

This lack was not because of scarce supply. A month after Burton

---

136 Ibid., 146.
137 Ibid., 194.

arrived, local citizens held a benefit to raise money to buy vegetables and other things for the prisoners at Fort Delaware. Not only were they denied permission to provide these things for the prisoners, but the meeting itself was raided by the local provost marshal and several men were taken to jail.

The reduced diet in the Union prisons was actually ordered from Washington as a reprisal for what they considered the ill treatment of Union prisoners held in Southern camps. The irony was that, even on the reduced rations ordered by the Federal government as punishment, the Confederate prisoners in the North were still eating almost as well as their brethren on the battle lines with Lee in Virginia or Joe Johnston in Georgia.

By the fall of 1864, as the reduced rations began to be felt throughout the Federal prison system, practices which, early on, had been novelties became common among the hungry prisoners. At Fort Delaware and other places like Johnson's Island and Elmira, the rodents which infested the prisons came to be seen as a natural protein source. The catching and eating of rats became widespread, and the carcasses became a standard item of the prison economy. One rat went for anywhere from four to ten cents, or could be traded for four chews of tobacco, one hair cut, or various other commodities.[138] Although he never mentioned it, there is a very good chance that Burton Warfield knew the taste of rat well before he left Fort Delaware. Some of the veterans said it was actually a lot like squirrel.

Food was not the only thing that captured the prisoners' interests, however. The normal drinking water supply being generally vile, every prison also had its amateur brewers who experimented with ways

---

138 Ibid., 245.

to produce a fermented drink out of the materials at hand. At Fort Delaware, they used molasses, cornmeal, and ginger to produce a drink which one inmate described as "villainous at best, but extra villainous when heated to a lukewarm temperature by hours under a vertical sun." He went on to explain that "the scarcity and putridity of the drinking water, and the predisposition to scurvy created by a diet of dry crackers and rusty salt meat, gives us all a craving for acid drinks, and many men sell their clothes to get funds to buy this 'small beer.'"[139]

Such were the conditions facing Burton Warfield as he settled into his new home.

---

139 Ibid., 195-196.

CHAPTER TWENTY-FIVE

# *Settling in for the Duration*

*"I am willing to endure anything almost for my country." (Burton Warfield)*

The arrival of Burton's group from Point Lookout on June 25, 1864, was recorded by one of Fort Delaware's most famous residents and diarists, Rev. Isaac W. K. Handy. One of the few civilian prisoners at the fort, Rev. Handy was a Presbyterian clergyman who had been arrested as a Southern sympathizer. Although he had earlier lived and worked in Delaware, when the war began he was serving a church in Portsmouth, Virginia. In July 1863, Rev. Handy and his family received a pass through the lines to visit family and friends near Delaware City, and during that visit, Rev. Handy was arrested, supposedly for some seditionist statements he had made in conversation, and taken to Fort Delaware. He had been there almost a year.[140]

As fate would have it, not only did Rev. Handy record the arrival of Burton's group—"About 650 men were introduced into the barracks in the course of the afternoon, crowding every 'shebang' very nearly to its utmost capacity"[141]—but he and a group of his friends also moved in next door to Burton on that same day. While Burton moved into Division 33, Rev. Handy and his group moved into Division 34. Just the

---

140 Rev. Isaac Handy, *United States Bonds, Duress by Federal Authorities* (Baltimore: Turnbull Brothers, 1874), hereafter referred to as the Diary of Isaac Handy. Copy supplied by The Ft. Delaware Society. The arrival of Burton's group is found on page 456.
141 Diary of Isaac Handy.

day before, they had been given permission to live in Division 34 and also use it as a "preaching room." The men had agreed to the inconvenience of having their living quarters converted into a church building whenever services were held, which was several times a week.

Rev. Handy's group was composed mostly of men who were trying to be good Christians in hard circumstances. Besides Rev. Handy, there were other men, who before the war had been preachers for different denominations or who had some religious training in the past. These and others shared the speaking assignments and conducted services, prayer meetings, and Bible classes in other divisions besides the regular services in Division 34. Just as on Johnson's Island, Burton would have found the Bible classes and services well attended.

These men, for the most part, put sectarian differences aside and tried to minister to the spiritual and physical needs of the prisoners as best they could. On any given day, the sermon might be given by Rev. Handy, a Presbyterian, if his health permitted, or by a Methodist or Baptist preacher, or by a respected layman. Some of these men, in their later years, would remember this time of hardship where all the Christians put aside their differences for the common good as the most spiritually rewarding time of their lives. It's very likely that Burton himself became part of this group, since in his later letters, he made several remarks about the religious services, classes, and baptisms he attended. He was, after all, very involved in his local congregation of restoration-minded Christians, known at the time as "Campbellites" after one of their best known preachers, Alexander Campbell, as well as the Church of Christ or Disciples of Christ or Christian Church. After the war, Burton served as an elder of the Cathey's Creek congregation, which still exists today in Maury County, Tennessee.

As Burton settled into his assigned place in Division 33, he took stock of his situation. If there was one common denominator in the Union prison system it was that wherever a prisoner was, money (Union greenbacks) made a huge difference in his quality of life, and unfortunately, Burton had almost none. What money he had at Johnson's Island had been in the form of credits on the prison books. It had been promised that these funds would be sent along after him, but he had seen none of it at Point Lookout, and now he was transferred again. Burton had already mentioned this problem, which could easily become a life or death issue, in his first letter from Fort Delaware, and it was still on his mind as he wrote his next letter, ten days later.

—⁓—

*Fort Delaware Del.*
*July 6th 1864*
*33 Division*
*My Dear Anna,*

*I do not know what to say nor how to say it. I have written you so often without receiving an answer. I fear they never reach you. It is just throwing away postage stamps, and being without money as I am it does not pay. I wrote you some time since to see Bro. Young and get him to send me some money by express. If he does not do it as he is owing me I can't but think he is treating me very coldly. I never in my life felt the need of money as I do now. My money at the island has not been heard from yet. We are on an island in the Delaware river 38 or 40 miles below Philadelphia. I can't tell how long we may stay here. It appears we are traveled around generally these times. I still hope to be in dixie soon. I think we will be exchanged after awhile. My health is tolerable good. How are you getting along—the corn crop, wheat, fruit, garden, etc. Write to me immediately let me know how you are getting along, and the news generally, neighbors, etc. Give my love to mother. Kiss the little ones for me. My kindest regards*

to all the neighbors. Receive to yourself the devotion of your affectionate
but unfortunate and imprisoned husband.

Burton Warfield

—∿∿—

It is obvious, from the tone of this letter, that Burton's spirits were
down. What he did not know was that Anna and a friend or relative
named Jones had already sent a box. Unfortunately, Anna had not yet
received Burton's letter telling of his move, so the box, mailed on July 5,
was sent to Point Lookout.[142] By the time he wrote his next letter, word
of the box had reached him, even if the box had not, and he sounded a
little guilty about his repeated requests for money.

—∿∿—

*Fort Delaware Del.*

*July 20th 1864*

*My Dear Anna*

*I received your letter of the 8th inst written at Wiley Jones, a few
days since. I have not received the box yet. It may be possible it will never
reach here. I am sorry you were put to so much trouble on my account.*

*It is true it would have been worth something to me here but not
enough probably to have justified me in giving you so much trouble. I
know the circumstances that surround you, the difficulties you labor
under, and the many inconveniences you are subject to. If I can only have
my health I can get along. My 12 months in prison is out. I will have to
reenlist for 12 months more, or during the war, which is the most probably.
But I am willing to endure anything almost for my country. I learn that
the cases of J. Briggs is ended. I am sorry to hear of the death of some of
our acquaintences in Georgia. I learn there are some cases of smallpox*

---

142 Adams Express receipt dated July 5, 1864, from the author's collection.

*Adams Express receipt for a package sent to Lt. Burton Warfield at Point Lookout Prison, July 5, 1864. Original in author's collection.*

here.[143] *My health is good. Write to me soon and often. Give me the news, tell me of the crops generally. It gives me much pleasure to know you have plenty to live upon, and thank God for his blessings. My love to all*

 *Yours truly*

 *Burton Warfield*

—⁓—

The fate of the box which Burton mentioned in this letter is not known. The handling of such parcels, which were so vital to a prisoner's life, were, if anything, more problematical than his letters. From Rev. Handy's writings, we know that a large shipment of packages was forwarded from Point Lookout on July 9, but this was much too soon (only four days) to contain Burton's box. Handy's comments about this shipment, however, point out that, in addition to being subject to pilfering during inspections, the slowness of the Union mail system caused other problems, too.

*Saturday, July 9, 1864*

 *A great many boxes have recently been forwarded from Point Lookout ... These boxes generally contain articles of provision, which being of a perishable nature, and so long delayed, are now perfectly useless. I am sure it would move the hearts of benevolent donors, if they could witness the disappointment of hungry "Rebs," sitting in groups around the open*

---

143 Fetzer and Mowday, *Unlikely Allies*, 116-119. Although vaccination for smallpox was increasingly common in the North, it was less so among Confederates, and the disease was a problem in many of the camps. In the summer and fall of 1863, a smallpox epidemic swept through Fort Delaware where it and associated diseases killed 1,200 men—almost half of the total who were to die there during the war. In response, the government set up a program to inoculate all the unvaccinated prisoners in order to eradicate smallpox in the prison. One way or another, then, Burton went home with a smallpox vaccination.

*boxes, knives in hand, scraping and paring, to secure a tidbit from the rotten mass."*[144]

Whatever was contained in Burton's box, it is very possible that Burton's own opinion, given in the letter above, was true: "It may be possible it will never reach here."

Overall, however, the mail system, for letters at least, seemed to be working well by this point in the war. Anna's next letter, which is unfortunately lost, took only eight days to travel from Franklin, Tennessee, to Fort Delaware. We do have Burton's answer, though, and it contains some interesting things.

—⁓—

*Fort Delaware*

*Aug 11th 1864*

*My Dear Anna*

*I received your letter written on the 23 of July yesterday. It was mailed at Franklin on the 2nd inst. I was glad to hear that you were all well and am sorry I can't be with you to enjoy those peach pies. I enjoy them to some extent in my imagination, and hope the time will yet come when we will be permitted to enjoy the fruits of domestic quietude around our own family hearth stone. We received an order yesterday prohibiting us from writing to anyone but our wives, parents, brothers and sisters. It does not interfer with me much. I have but few corispondence.*[145] *I wrote to Amalick yesterday morning. I do not know whether it will go or not. If you see him tell him about it and tell him to write to me and if I do not answer his*

---

144 Diary of Isaac Handy, 477.

145 Ibid., 500. The issuance of this order is confirmed by Rev. Handy in his diary entry of August 10, 1864, exactly the date which Burton gives.

*letters he must excuse me. The weather is very warm and offensive. I have had for several days one of my old fashioned colds. Getting better. When was John Pipkins captured and what prison did he die in?*[146] *I have not heard any thing from Bob Maberry or Perryman.*[147] *You must be mistaken about where they are. Capt. Polk saw Perryman at Camp Chase.*[148] *He did not see Maberry. Write to me as often as you can. Remember me to all the neighbors and friends. My love to Mother. Kiss the little ones for me. May the blessings of heaven rest upon you all is the sincere desire of*

*Your devoted husband*

*Burton Warfield*

—∙∙∙—

This letter found Burton in a somewhat better mood after receiving word from home. The news from the farm seemed to have been good, and thanks to Anna's letter, he had at least the imagination of her peach pies to cheer him. His comments about the weather came as no surprise, August often being an oppressive time, but this hot spell seemed to have been worse than normal. The Rev. Handy, probably lying in his bunk only a few yards away in Division 34 as Burton was writing this letter in Division 33, spent his complete diary entry for this date complaining about the heat. He began this way: "Thursday, [August] 11th—I don't know when I have ever before experienced such a day as this. The heat has been almost intolerable." To make matters even worse, Handy could

---

146 Private Pipkins was a friend, but a member of another unit, the Nineteenth Tennessee Cavalry (sometimes called the 9th), commanded by Burton's old commander, Col. Jake Biffle.

147 These two men were privates in Burton's unit, Company "A," First Tennessee Cavalry.

148 This officer was Capt. James H. Polk, commander of Company "E" in Burton's regiment. Captain Polk was the nephew of Confederate Gen. Leonidas Polk, who had been killed two months before in Georgia.

see the ice house from his window in Division 34, but as he said, "not a pound was to be had, either for money or entreaty."[149]

Of special interest in this letter are Burton's references to several fellow prisoners. The long rows of barracks, called "cow sheds" by the inmates, were broken up into rooms, or divisions. As mentioned before, the divisions were numbered, but they were also named for the home state of the men who occupied them. According to the later memory of one prisoner, there were at least two Tennessee divisions.[150] By now, Burton had been at Fort Delaware forty-eight days and certainly was acquainted with most of the other Tennessee men, especially the ones from his own unit or county.

Of the men named in this letter, John Pipkins was a neighbor or friend in another unit, the Nineteenth Tennessee Cavalry, and Bob Maberry and Perryman were enlisted men in Burton's own company where he was second in command. Naturally, the fate of these men who had served under him and were probably also friends or neighbors, was of great interest, but the last man mentioned by name is the most interesting and the most historically significant.

Capt. James Hilliard Polk is the officer mentioned in Burton's letter as having seen Perryman at Camp Chase, another Union prison at Columbus, Ohio. Captain Polk was the commander of Company "E" in Burton's regiment and a member of the most prominent family in Maury County, Tennessee. The son of George Washington Polk, nephew of Confederate Lt. Gen. Leonidas Polk, and a cousin of former president James K. Polk, Captain Polk was captured six months after Burton and had come to Fort Delaware by a different route. Unfortunately, in

---

149 Diary of Isaac Handy, 501-502.
150 Speer, *Portals to Hell*, 146.

a few days, he would leave Fort Delaware as part of a group of POWs which would become known as the Immortal 600.

In the summer of 1864, tales of the plight of Northern prisoners held by the South raised cries of outrage from the public and in Congress, and resulted in the authorities intentionally reducing the rations in Northern prisons in "retaliation." In fact, the problem was not with the Confederate government. It was quite willing to return their Union prisoners on almost any terms. It was actually the Northern government and the Union military command that decided to leave the Union prisoners to their fate rather than take them back and relieve the burden on the Confederacy. When Jefferson Davis ordered that a group of over six thousand prisoners from Andersonville be taken to the nearest Union garrison and offered for parole, with nothing asked in return but that a receipt be signed for them, the Union Commander at St. Augustine, Florida, turned them away. General Grant and others had made the deliberate decision to leave the Northern prisoners in the hands of the Confederate government, which by this time could not even feed its own people, in order to speed up its collapse.[151] In the middle of all this, a situation arose in Charleston, South Carolina, which would affect Burton's friend, Captain Polk, and many others.

In the summer of 1864, Maj. Gen. Samuel Jones was the Confederate commander of the Department of South Carolina, based in Charleston. On the Union side, shelling the city every day, was his opposite number, Union Maj. Gen. John G. Foster. During this time, the Confederates were moving a number of prisoners from Andersonville to other places, and some passed through Charleston. When General

---

151 Maurial P. Joslyn, *Immortal Captives* (Shippensburg, PA: White Mane Publishing Company, 1996), 34.

Foster learned, from escaped prisoners, that there were six hundred Union POWs being held in the town, he accused the Confederates of using them as human shields, placing them in the line of fire of the Union artillery, and requested six hundred Southern prisoners to be placed under the Confederate guns as retaliation. The request was granted, and on the day that Burton wrote this last letter, the word reached Fort Delaware.

In any prison, military or civilian, one of the most efficient operations is the prisoner grapevine, so by the next morning, the rumor mill was in full swing. The word was that six hundred officers were to be taken South for exchange immediately. On the following morning, August 13, the names of six hundred Confederate officers were called, including Burton's friend Captain Polk, and a week later, on August 20, they were marched aboard the Yankee steamer *Crescent City*. Spirits were high among the officers selected, even though they had all heard that they might be placed under the fire of Confederate batteries around Charleston as retaliation.[152] Most believed that, even if this were true, they would still be exchanged in the end.

After eighteen miserable days sailing down the East coast, 560 of the men were landed on Morris Island,[153] one of the islands commanding the approaches to Charleston Harbor, and put into a stockade between two Union artillery emplacements, Battery Wagner and Battery Gregg. For the next forty-five days, they lived there while the artillery dueled with the Southern guns at Fort Sumter and Fort Moultrie. Any Confederate shells that fell short of Wagner or went long over Gregg ran the risk of

---

152 Joslyn, *Immortal Captives*, 59, and Diary of Isaac Handy, 504, 505, 514.
153 Joslyn, *Immortal Captives*, 81. Forty men had already been sent to the Federal military hospital at Beauford, South Carolina.

killing their own men. On October 21, the Yankees gave up the exercise, moved the remaining 549 men out of the stockade and transported them to Fort Pulaski, near Savannah, Georgia.[154]

During the time the prisoners were in place, shelling took place almost every day. Union guards on the walls were killed by falling shells, and several soldiers in the Union fortifications were also killed by the Confederate bombardment, but due to what the Confederate prisoners were convinced was divine intervention, not one of the POWs was killed. Numerous shells landed within the compound, and fragments often littered the pathways, but the only deaths among the Immortal 600 were due to disease and malnutrition. Capt. James H. Polk was eventually exchanged at Charleston and survived the war.

---

154 Ibid., 136.

## CHAPTER TWENTY-SIX

## *The Second Winter*

*"Cold and inhospital winter is coming upon us with long strids."*
(Burton Warfield)

A t Fort Delaware, late summer turned into fall, with some merciful relief from the hot weather, but early September was not a time of good news for the Confederates who were following the course of the war as best they could from inside a Union prison. After fighting around the outskirts for almost six weeks, Confederate forces evacuated Atlanta on September 1, and a Union army under Gen. William T. Sherman marched into the city the next day. A week later, Burton received his next letter from home.

—⁓—

*Stony Point*
*Sept. 9th 1864*
*Dear Burton,*

*It is with pleasure that I embrace this opportunity of sending you a few lines. We are all well. I am anxiously expecting a letter from you. I recieved two last week. —have written two or three since but did not secceed in getting them to town. I have saw Dick and Alonzo since I wrote. All of King's [Kinzer's] company[155] have been home. I saw Capt. [Kinzer]*

---

155 I believe the name "King" in this letter is an error in the transcription from the original. There is no record of an officer named King ever serving in Burton's regiment. It is almost certain that the name here is actually "Kinzer" as I have indicated in brackets. *(note cont. next page)*

He looks hearty as ever. I expect they have been captured. Since they left a great many of Wheeler's men were captured. Mr. Mabery has heard from Bob. We were disappointed with our big meeting. preacher did not come but Bro Lipscomb commences one here tomorrow. He will be sure to come I think.[156] I heard from Cousin Bill. he said he had sent you $50.00 by express let us know if you did not get it and he will send you more. I will close.

> Yours as ever
> Anna Warfield.[157]

—⁂—

In this letter, Anna mentioned to Burton that his old company had been home recently. The name transcribed as "King" is almost certainly "Kinzer" in the original. If so, the "Alonzo" Anna mentioned would be her younger brother, Samuel Alonzo Worley, a private in that company. This is all shown to be quite possible by a regimental history. During this time—late August/early September 1864—Burton's old unit was, in fact, engaged in a movement from Knoxville to a point near Nashville and from there south to Florence, Alabama, taking them through Maury County.[158] Evidently, even though they were in Yankee territory, some of the local men were allowed to stop by their homes for a time, and this is what Anna reported. Her fear that they had all been captured,

---

155 *(cont.)* Capt. George M.V. Kinzer was Burton's company commander, both in the old Second Battalion Tennessee Cavalry and in the Sixth Tennessee Cavalry (Wheeler), and was also a friend and neighbor. JRK

156 This preacher, who replaced the one who failed to show up to hold their meeting, was David Lipscomb of Nashville. He was well known in Middle Tennessee as a Restoration Movement preacher, writer, and educator. Lipscomb University, which he helped found after the war, stands today on land that was once part of his farm on the southern edge of Nashville.

157 This letter (September 9, 1864) is present only in the *Historic Maury* collection.

158 *Tennesseans in the Civil War*, Part 1, 67

however, was unfounded. Neither Captain Kinzer nor her brother Alonzo was captured. They both survived the war, finally surrendering in North Carolina, and returning home.

Burton's next letter is only dated "October 1864," but it is obvious that fall was well advanced. On October 9, Rev. Handy began his daily diary entry with this passage:

*A very cold night. Suffered much, my blood being too thin to be heated by the covering at command. Others have been complaining, and the cry is "How shall we stand it this winter?"*[159]

From the tone of this letter, however, it was obvious that something more than the prospect of winter weather was on Burton's mind. It seemed that the lack of mail or word from anyone outside his family was causing him to wonder what opinion his friends and neighbors back home really had of him, and whether they were truly committed to the cause for which he has fought. This is a theme which has been present, from time to time up to now, and will return again. In this letter, for a few lines, he became philosophical and abandoned the normal simple sentences for some flights of florid Victorian prose. That style might seem strange, coming from a Tennessee farmer, but he fell into it occasionally when he wrote passionately about something, or in this case, indulged in a little self pity.

—⁂—

*Fort Delaware, Del*
*Oct 1864*
*My Dear Wife,*

---

159 Diary of Isaac Handy, 597.

Cold and inhospital winter is coming upon us with long strids. The green and beautiful shores of the Delaware have put on a darker mantle for the approaching winter. While the green foliage of the sunny south are faned by balmy breeses, bleak and dreary winds come to us here on our island home and swell the turbid waves of the Delaware. But it is an uncommon wind that blows no good. I have pondered much upon home and loved ones there since I last wrote you. I know that I have a friend in you and my dear mother, but beyond that I know not whether I have a friend in Tenn. Are they friends, who, in your prosperity come to you with sweet smiles and flatering words, but in your adversity are as cold and silent as the grave? Are they so subjugated that they fear to open their lips to bless or give a word of comfort or a friendly word to one whom they once recognised as a friend! Is it because I am a rebel? Is it because I am a trator? (As some of the oppressors of our country call all those who are struggling only for their rights and independence.) Or is [it] because they are so devoted to Lincoln in the prosecution of this unholy war that they treat as enemies those they once hailed as friends. Is it so? God forbid. We have religious services here every day. All denominations unite with perfect concord and harmony. Frequent acceptance to the church. Some are sprinkled others are buried in the waves of the delaware. We have prairs in each division every night after which we retire to our cold and hard couches to dream of bygone days and a furture reunion with, and the embraces of, loved ones at home. I am well, and in good spirits as to the final result of our cause. My love to all. Write often.

Goodbye

[Your] devoted husband

—꘏—

Burton's feelings of abandonment were tied directly to the erratic nature of his contact with home and his fear that it was caused by more than just the Union postal system. It was easy for him, in prison and living in conditions that would probably make the circumstances of his poorest acquaintances back home seem like luxury, to feel forgotten and unappreciated. Stuck on a dreary mud flat seven hundred miles from home, guarded by enemies, living in grim circumstances on near starvation rations, and with little hope of release anytime soon, Burton can probably be forgiven for feeling that he deserved better from some of his friends and neighbors back home. Once he got that out of his system, however, he returned to a subject he had mentioned many times—the religious life within the prison.

Some men in prison embraced religion as a means to get through a trying time, but for many others, like Burton, faith had long been a fundamental part of their lives. For these, trying times only strengthened convictions they already held. The idea that hundreds of ragged, dirty soldiers who were subsisting on hard tack crackers, potted meat, and whatever else they could buy or trap from the countryside would meet almost daily for religious services might strike us as hard to believe, but it was true.

About two months before Burton wrote this letter, a group of men, including Rev. Handy, formally organized the Fort Delaware Christian Association, complete with a constitution, by-laws, and officers. Burton was almost certainly involved with this group and might even have served on one of the standing committees, which before he was released had expanded to include groups concerned with: State of the Church, Introduction, Education, Finance, Religious Reading, Devotional Exercises, Sick and Destitute, Order and Arrangements, and Music.[160]

---

160 Diary of Isaac Handy, 491 and Prison newspaper *Fort Delaware Prison Times*, Vol. 1, No. 1, April 1865.

Burton's comment about having "prairs [sic] in each division every night" was not just a personal habit. Organized evening prayers were the result of a formal proposal by the Christian Association. It was voted on in each division and was carried with very few dissenters. After the proposition had passed, some divisions even reported a decrease in the gambling activity.[161] It's also obvious from Burton's comments that, just as at Johnson's Island, the degree of tolerance among the adherents of various denominations far exceeded anything he had experienced before the war. When he mentioned the "frequent acceptance to the church," he went on to say that some were baptized by being "buried in the waves of the Delaware" while others were sprinkled, even though sprinkling would never have been accepted as valid baptism in his congregation back home. In the desperate circumstances in which these men found themselves, the concept of who was considered a Christian was probably broader than they had ever considered before, and for many, would ever consider again.

Anna's next letter came near the end of the month and along with the usual money and clothes worries, contained news from home, showing that religious activity and controversy were alive and well in the Warfields' little corner of Maury County, Tennessee, also.

—⚹—

*Stony Point*

*October 28th 1864*

*My dear Burton*

*Again I take the priviledge to address you. I haven't recieved a letter this week. I have not ascertained yet whether I can send you any money, will though in a few days. You think I have use for the little that I make. Its of no*

---

161 Diary of Isaac Handy, 588ff.

*consequence to me when you are needing it so bad. I heard a few days ago that there was not going to be any more clothes or money sent to prisoners. I hope it is a false report. I was in hopes you wouldn't have to spent another [winter] there. Cold climate will not agree with you. I have been to pa's to a big meeting since I wrote to you. Bro Trimble and Picken preached. They both think it's wrong for Christians to fight. Bro Picken is the same Jim Picken that went to school in Hampshire he is a brother to Andrew. I think he is a smart man He was chaplain in the army 12 months and saw he was wrong and came out of it.[162] Had three aditions. Callie Johnson was one of them. Grandma went down when I did and she is going to stay a week or two. It nearly killed her to think about you undergoing so many hardships. She often says she's afraid she won't live to see you, should you be so fortunate as to get home again. She has very good health now. Kaeiser is well. Minnie has been sick three or four days. She is better today. I want you to write to Wiley J. Stratton N.Y. He has sent clothes to prisoners or has management of it someway. He is a brother to Mrs. Egrus at Hampshire. Alice Biffle said that her uncle Bill was going to get clothes that way and told me to be sure and tell you to write to him for clothes. The children have gathered a great many chestnuts. They are very fine this year. Kaeiser goes out every day. He has two or three qts. for you. They save a great many things for you. I believe I told you that Martha had another girl. It's three weeks old.*

*I will close for the present. May the Lord bless and protect you.*

*Goodby*

*Yours truly Anna[163]*

---

162 It must have been a little strained for these two preachers to speak against the involvement of Christians in the war when there was probably not a single family in the audience who did not have a husband or father or son or nephew or cousin either actively serving in the Confederate army or, like Burton, in a Yankee prison.

163 This letter (October 28, 1864) is present only in the *Historic Maury* collection.

—⁓—

Surely, Burton was glad to hear the latest news from home and know his family was safe and well, even though the thought of his worried mother must have been hard. Of course, we can only guess how much those three quarts of chestnuts his five-year-old son was saving for him would have been worth on the open market in the Fort Delaware bull pen. Unfortunately, events were already in motion to interrupt Burton and Anna's communication for several months.

## CHAPTER TWENTY-SEVEN
## *Battles Close To Home*

*"If we are to die, let us die like men."*
*(Maj. Gen. Patrick Ronayne Cleburne)*

The military campaign in which Burton Warfield was captured in July, 1863, also resulted in the Union forces controlling Middle Tennessee. This meant, of course, that Burton's wife and family and farm had been in "occupied territory" for the last sixteen months. As much as he might have wished that his home state and county were still Southern territory, having the Yankees in control had its advantages. Better that than having Anna and his children and mother in the middle of an area which was constantly changing hands and being fought over like some parts of Virginia. As we've seen, the Yankees even provided reliable postal service which allowed Burton to get letters and parcels from home. As November, 1864, began, however, all that was about to be interrupted.

After capturing Atlanta at the beginning of September, Union Gen. William T. Sherman spent the next six weeks or so trying to pin down what was left of the Confederate defenders, now under the command of Gen. John Bell Hood, while the Southerners tried to draw Sherman north from Atlanta and destroy what they could of the railroad, which was the Yankees' supply line back into Tennessee. At the same time, Sherman was trying to sell his boss, Ulysses S. Grant, on an audacious plan to move from Atlanta across the state to Savannah.

By early November, Sherman had given up chasing Hood around

northwest Georgia and northeast Alabama. He had already sent Gen. George Thomas back to Nashville to defend Middle Tennessee, and now he prepared to take the rest of his army from Atlanta toward the coast. Sherman intended, as he told Grant, "to make Georgia howl!" and he certainly did. For Hood's part, he had two choices. He could try and follow Sherman and nip at his heels all the way to the Atlantic Ocean, or he could strike out on his own. Not surprisingly, he chose the second option. On November 16, Sherman left Atlanta with 60,000 men, beginning what would be called his "March to the Sea." Five days later, Hood took his own army across the Tennessee River at Florence, Alabama, bound for Nashville, just over one hundred miles to the north.[164] To counter this move, George Thomas sent a force of 25,000 men under Union Gen. John Schofield to meet him south of the Duck River.[165]

George Thomas, the Union commander at Nashville, was something of a rarity in the Civil War—a native Virginian who remained with the Union. At West Point, he had picked up the nickname "Old Slow Trot" because of his deliberate methods, but once the war began, he quickly proved his worth. Although he sometimes frustrated his superiors with his lack of speed, he had never lost a battle, and more than once had saved the rest of the army by holding a position when others broke and ran. Because of this kind of performance in one major battle, he now had a new nickname, "The Rock of Chickamauga." After the Battle of Atlanta, Sherman said of him, "George Thomas is, you know, slow, but true as steel."[166] This was the man General Sherman trusted to defend

---

164 Wiley Sword, *The Confederacy's Last Hurrah*, (Lawrence, KS: University Press of Kansas, 1992), 72-74.
165 James Lee McDonough and Thomas L. Connelly, *Five Tragic Hours*, (Knoxville, TN: University Of Tennessee Press, 1983), 27.
166 Sword, *Confederacy's Last Hurrah*, 77.

Tennessee while he marched through Georgia.

General Schofield's mission was not to defeat Hood's Southern army, but to delay it as much as he could so as to give Thomas time to gather forces for the defense of Nashville. Schofield was to force Hood to slow down and engage him at every opportunity, but then to fall back without getting cut off. With Nathan Bedford Forrest commanding 6,000 or more Confederate cavalry, that would soon prove to be easier said than done.

Over the next week, John Schofield had his hands full. He formed a defensive line on the Duck River at Columbia, but was almost cut off when a force of cavalry and infantry crossed the river and got behind him. Only a gallant stand by some of his troops at Spring Hill, combined with confusion in the Confederate chain of command and the coming of darkness, allowed him to escape northward up the Columbia Pike during the night of November 29 to the relative safety of the existing works at Franklin. There the Union troops set to work improving their position and waited for Hood to arrive.

When he woke up on the morning of November 30 to find that the entire Union army had escaped during the night, John Bell Hood, who had a useless arm from Gettysburg and had lost a leg at Chickamauga, was said to be "Wrathy as a rattlesnake, striking at everything."[167] No amount of anger or blame on subordinates could bring back the chance that had eluded them, however, so there was nothing to do but follow the Yankees north. By early afternoon, the first Southern troops came through the saddle in the low range of hills just south of the town of Franklin and got their first look at the Northern defenses. What they saw was not encouraging. When Hood arrived, he rode to Winstead Hill and pulled out his field glasses. Two miles away stood the Union fortifications.

---

167 Ibid., 156.

Sometime after 2:00 p.m., in a conference with his commanders, Hood announced that they would attack immediately. Even though all his subordinates argued against the plan, and in spite of the fact that one corps of his army and almost all his artillery were still on the road south of town, Hood would not be swayed. Because of the numbers of troops involved, it took over an hour to get them in position, and all the while, the Union soldiers watched from behind their fortifications. These Confederate troops were all veterans, and they had no illusions about what it meant to assault well-dug-in troops over open ground. They had been defenders themselves often enough, so they knew that many of them would shortly be dead. All the Southern chaplains were quickly loaded down with watches, letters, and keepsakes for delivery to loved ones back home, but in the end, it would do little good since many of the chaplains would be dead, too.

Even if they weren't optimistic about their chances, however, the Confederates still had their pride. Just after 4:00 p.m., the Union defenders were astonished to see rank upon rank of soldiers in gray and butternut move out of the trees and form up as if on parade, complete with battle flags and even bands, which marched into battle with them. One veteran, years later remarking on the courage even of the musicians, said that at Franklin "the tooters went in with the shooters." Knowing how strong their position was, the Union troops never dreamed that the enemy would be so foolhardy as to assault them head on. Amazed, they scrambled to their places behind the log barricades and watched the spectacle. The Confederates' charge at Franklin would involve more men than Pickett's Charge at Gettysburg, advancing over twice the distance with almost no artillery support, and against a position where many of the Union defenders were armed with repeating rifles. The results were tragically predicable.

The next five hours saw some of the most horrendous fighting of the entire war. Veterans on both sides later said they had never seen so much carnage in so small an area. In one of the most famous accounts by a veteran of the battle, Sam Watkins of the First Tennessee Infantry, who had been present for every battle fought by the Army of Tennessee said simply,"I cannot describe it. It beggars description ... Would to God I had never witnessed such a scene!"[168]

By daylight the next day, the Yankees had pulled out for Nashville, leaving Hood in possession of the field, but with over 6,000 casualties. Even more serious were the losses in the officers' ranks. Since most Civil War officers led from the front, they fell in large numbers. Six general officers were killed and five more wounded and put out of action. As many as five divisions were essentially decapitated, their command structure being almost wiped out in front of the Union fortifications.

Over the next few days, Hood's army pulled itself together, reorganized what was left, and marched on after the retreating Yankees toward Nashville. For two weeks, they waited outside the Union lines, suffering from a winter storm and preparing for the attack they knew must come. With only about 24,000 men camped out in the open and shivering from the cold, the Confederates faced over twice that number, safe and warm behind the fortifications of the city. Whenever George Thomas decided to come out and fight, the odds were overwhelmingly in his favor.

On December 15 the waiting was over. Under the cover of fog, the Union troops came out of the fortifications of Nashville and attacked, and by the next afternoon, Hood's army was in full retreat. Only brave rear guard actions by a few units saved the army from complete destruction. By December 27, the remnants of the army were back across the Tennessee

---

168 Watkins, *Co. Aytch*, 232.

River in north Alabama. In his report to his commander, Gen. Thomas J. Wood, commanding the troops who pursued the Confederates during their retreat, told General Thomas that he should "Feel confident that Hood has not taken across the Tennessee River more than half the men he brought across it; that not more than one-half of those taken out are armed; that he lost three fourths of his artillery and that, for rout, demoralization, even disintegration, the condition of his command is without parallel in this war."[169]

The remnants of this once proud army continued to resist in a few places for the next four months, but after Franklin and Nashville, the Army of Tennessee was finished as an effective fighting force. During this time, the armies passed within fifteen miles of Burton and Anna's farm, but there is no record of any fighting in that area. The action cut Anna off from any mail service, and surely caused some anxious moments, as there was almost certainly some movement of troops, probably cavalry, through the neighborhood, but as far as we know, she and the family came through alright. Other than Burton's statement in his first letter of 1865 about communications being cut, nothing is ever mentioned about the great battles that had gone on so close to home.[170]

---

169 Paul H. Stockdale, *Death of an Army*, (Murfreesboro, TN: Southern Heritage Press, 1992), 162.

170 My short account of Hood's campaign through Burton and Anna's neighborhood in late 1864 is taken from sources already cited. McDonough and Connelly's work is the classic study of the Battle of Franklin, while Sword's is the most complete study of the entire campaign. JRK

## Chapter Twenty-Eight
### *"Sturn Reality"*

From Burton's next letter, it is clear that he had been following the Confederates' campaign in Middle Tennessee and knew that writing home or expecting a letter from Anna was futile while the fighting was going on. By the end of the first week of January, however, he had heard that Hood's army had been defeated and retreated back into Alabama, so he decided to try and resume contact.

———

*Fort Delaware*

*Jan 7th 1865*

*My Dear Anna*

*It has been a long time since I heard from you, but I have endured it with a good deal of patience knowing that communication with home was cut off for a while. But as it is now opened again I am uneasy and anxious to hear from you. I have not written to you for some time for several reasons. I knew that communication was cut and it would be useless to write and I have not the means to get paper, envelops, stamps and all. Another Christmas has fallen and found me in prison surrounded with snow and ice and the fourth one I have been denied the happy priviledge of being at home and enjoying the society of loved ones. I am sorry to inform you that I have not received any clothing yet. I could get some any time if I could get a permit to have them sent to me. The weather is very cold [but]* not so cold as it was at the Island last winter. I hope you will write to me soon and give me all the news. Bill Sullivan has not sent me the postage stamps you gave him for me. My health is tolerable good. You spoke of John White going to Rock island to see his brothers. I will advise you not to think of sending him here. You would incur a useless expense and ten chances to one whether he could get to see me should he come. Give my love to mother. Remember me to all inquerring friends. I wish you a happy new year. Hoping to hear from you soon. I remain your devoted husband

    Burton Warfield

—⚮—

Unfortunately for Burton, contact with home from now until his release would prove sporadic at best. Whether he received a prompt answer to this letter, we don't know. Anna's letter dated October 28, 1864, is the last one to survive. Burton's almost constant worry from this point on would be the lack of word from home. From now until his release, he only acknowledged receiving two more letters from Anna.

By now, Burton had been a prisoner of war for eighteen months, and his life had settled into a monotonous routine. In the summer, he fought the insects and the mud and tried to keep cool, and in the winter, he fought the snow and ice and tried to keep warm, and, at all times, he tried to get something to eat. As mentioned in his letter, clothes and warmth were most on his mind. The divisions at Fort Delaware had no insulation and were made of rough wood, so the winter wind off the river blew through in dozens of places. Each division or room, which held about four hundred men, was provided with two stoves, but their heat, even when going full blast, could only be felt a few feet away. This gave rise to a type of prisoner known as "Stove Rats." Burton must have known them well. At times, he might even have been one himself.

Every division had its stove rats. They would crowd around the stove, blocking what little heat there was, while the rest of the men shivered in their bunks, trying to keep warm with whatever clothes and blankets they could gather. Some days, when the cold was really intense, some of the other prisoners would rebel against the stove rats, as described by one inmate over forty years later:

*Those who crowded around the stove continually were dubbed stove rats. On very cold days, those who spent most of their time on their bunks trying to keep warm would get down in the passway between the bunks, form in columns of one or two, with as many in the rear as wished to participate, and charge the stove rats. The hindmost would push those in front until the stove was cleared. The rear ones would then take possession at the stove until another column would form and make a countercharge, when the rear ones of this column would take their turn at the stove.[171]*

Day after freezing day went by for Burton and the thousands of other Confederate prisoners in the island prison with little good news to cheer them. Finally, in February, word came of another possible exchange. Unlike so many such rumors, this one turned out to be true, and over one thousand men were actually loaded aboard a steamer called the *Cassandra* and sent off to Virginia.[172] Suddenly, things were looking up, and more of the same was expected. For once, Burton, who was due for a little good luck, got a break. A few weeks later, when he next wrote to Anna, he had some really good news.

---

171 W. H. Moon, "Prison Life at Fort Delaware," *Confederate Veteran*, (Nashville, TN, 1907) XV, 213. Quoted in an article by Nancy Travis Keen.
172 Fetzer and Mowday, *Unlikely Allies*, 132.

—m—

Fort Delaware Del.

March 7, 1865

My Dear Anna

I cannot forego the pleasure of pening you a few more lines upon the eve of my departure from Fort Delaware. I am going to the sunny south and it may be many days er you hear from me again. I may be declared exchanged on arriving at Richmond and go immediately to the field, or I may remain on parole for two or three months. In the latter case I cannot go home, but may go to some of our relatives in Alabama. I hope an opportunity may present itself by which I can hear from you. Should you have a opportunity be sure and write to me. I will do the same. I would be glad to get a letter from you before I leave. I can but commend you to the goodness and mercy of an all wise providence who will protect and comfort his people. I commit myself, my country, and my all into his hands. I know that you have a great and responsible duty resting upon you, and as I am not permitted to share that responsibility at present it makes it more onerous upon you. I would be unhappy had I not implicit confidence in your goodness, and your wisdom and judgement in rearing our little ones, and you have mothers council to whom I look with ( ? ) and pleasure as having instilled into my bosom in my childhood principals of truth and ( ? ) that have ever remained with me through trials and temptations. I hope that brighter and happier days are in store for us. Farewell. May heavens blessings rest upon you. Your devoted and affectionate husband.

Burton Warfield

—m—

This time, so it seems, Burton's name had been called, and possibly paperwork made out, as well, stating that he was to be exchanged. Having the paperwork in hand, however, was not the same as actually getting off the island, as Burton was to find out. Larger events were in control. The Confederacy was crumbling. By now, Richmond had been under siege for almost ten months. Everyone knew that it was just a matter of time, and not much time at that. Because of all these reasons, Burton Warfield, a technically paroled prisoner, still continued to sit on his island in the Delaware River. Since he had told Anna that he was to leave immediately for the "sunny South," he also got no letters from home. His next letter was written after he had been waiting a month for the exchange that would never come.

—⁓—

*Fort Delaware*
*April 4, 1865*
*My Dear Anna*

*I have been paroled four weeks today and have not got off yet. The exchange is suspended for a while. I fear I will have to stay here some time yet. I get no letters from you now. Have you quit writing to me? I would be glad to hear from you again. How are you getting on gardening. I imagine you and mother working in the garden, and vegitation putting on its robe of green and every thing looking cheerfull this bright April morning as of yore and again immagination reflects you not as cheerful as I would wish, distressed with cares and troubles. God help you, as for myself I have to deal with sturn [sic] reality. I know what I feel, what I wish, and what I fear. Write to me soon give me all the news, how you are getting on and what your prospects for the present are. We have just heard of the fall of Richmond. I hope exchange will soon be resumed. My love to mother, and the little ones. Tell me whether Kaeiser and Minnie look like they did two years ago. Have they grown much. God love and protect you.*

*Your husband*
*Burton*

—⁀⁀⁀—

It is easy to understand why Burton would prefer to imagine Anna and his mother working in the garden on a bright April morning. That's certainly more enjoyable than dealing with what he referred to as "sturn reality," the fall of Richmond, of which he had just learned, being only the latest example.

The capital of the Confederacy had been in a state of partial siege since June 1864, when General Grant brought his forces up in a long semicircle that stretched from northeast of the city southward past Petersburg. Lee had drawn up a defensive line to face him, and there matters stood for the last ten months. Numerous small actions had taken place all through the fall and winter, but neither side could gain the critical advantage until now.

Beginning on April 1, Grant began a series of attacks south of Petersburg, which forced Lee and what was left of his army, as well as President Jefferson Davis and the Confederate government to flee to the west. On April 3, Federal troops entered the Confederate capital. In this case, Burton and his fellow prisoners didn't learn of the fall of their capital through a newspaper story or rumor. Their captors were only too happy to announce the news themselves. Within a few hours of the fall of Richmond, the news was on the telegraph wires. When the message came to the office in Delaware City, on the western shore of the river, early in the afternoon, it was rushed over to the fort.

Gen. Albin Schoepf, Fort Delaware's commander, read the dispatch in silence and then called in his officers. He wanted to announce this news in a spectacular way. He ordered all gun crews to load their cannons and stand by for his signal. It was almost sundown before they were ready. Inside the fort, Schoepf stood in the center of the parade ground and waited. When he received the sign from all his battery commanders that they were loaded and ready, he gave them a signal and 156 cannons, that had never fired a shot in anger, were all touched off at once. In that instant, all the prisoners knew that something important had happened. Soon, Union officers arrived at the prison camp and read the dispatch in every division. In the prisoners' compound, the mood was somber, but in the Yankee camp, there was a very large party, with many a hangover the next morning.[173]

---

173 Ibid., 133-135.

# CHAPTER TWENTY-NINE
## Going Home

*"I have despaired of our success for the first time since the war commenced."*
*(Burton Warfield)*

**A**fter hearing about the fall of Richmond, I'm sure Burton wasn't the only prisoner who woke up the next morning and decided to write a letter home. Unfortunately, there was worse news to come. On April 10, 1865, the guns of the fort began firing again, and fired at intervals all day—225 rounds in all—to celebrate Lee's surrender at Appomattox the day before. Just as with the announcement a week before, the next day, Burton sat down and wrote another letter. Aside from his constant complaint about the lack of letters from home, it's clear that Burton had finally accepted the fact that the "Cause" was lost.

———

*Fort Delaware*

*April 11, 1865*

*My Dear Anna*

*Have you forgotten me? Or what is the cause of your silence? I write to you regularly but no answer or word from you. A gloom of sadness overspreads us at present. I have despaired of our success for the first time since the war commenced. Gen Lee, the greatest and best man of the age, has surrendered. The army of Tenn now under Gen Johnston will have to surrender if it has not already done so.[174] What is to be done with us I*

---

174 What was left of the Army of Tennessee under Gen. Joe Johnston held out for another two weeks, surrendering to General Sherman in North Carolina on April 26.

*know not. I hope to see you soon. In the meantime write to me. I would*
*write you a longer letter but I fear you do not get my letters. My health is*
*not as good as it has been. Nothing more than a cold though. Give my love*
*to all, write soon.*

    *Yours as ever, Burton*

—⁂—

Two more weeks went by, during which many momentous events
occurred, before Burton wrote his next letter. Most important of all,
on the evening of April 14, President Abraham Lincoln was shot by
John Wilkes Booth, while attending a play at Ford's Theater, the first
American president to be assassinated while in office. For whatever
reason, Burton mentioned nothing at all about the president's death
in his next letter, written ten days after the assassination.

—⁂—

*Fort Delaware*
*April 24th 1865*
*My Dear Anna,*

    *I have not heard from you since the 1st of March. I am in a state of*
*great anxiety and uneasiness about you. I write to you regularly at least*
*once a week. It is a buisey season now and the people go to town but*
*seldom and I know you have but few chances to send a letter to the office.*
*A great gloom overshadows us now. Our fond hopes of independence are*
*all most crushed out. The great cause for which we have been strugling*
*for four years to be abandoned and ourselves humiliated. I have nothing*
*to regret. I have been honest in my views and still believe that we were in*
*the right. I want to see you very bad. But whether I will be permitted to*
*return to my home and to the loved ones there is a question to be decided*
*yet. My health is tolerable good at present. Our rations are short. Give*
*my love to mother. Remember me to the neighbors and friends. Hoping*

*to hear from you soon I remain as ever*
>   *Yours*
>   *Burton*

—⁓—

Burton Warfield's next letter from captivity was written five days later. His mood had changed considerably, and for the first time in a long while, there was an attempt at humor. It seemed that, now that the war was really over, he had made his peace with the situation and was looking forward to a brighter future. Also, in this next letter, he makes a statement which, taken together with a comment from the previous letter, expresses the feelings of thousands and thousands of his comrades now that the war had ended. They were willing to admit defeat on the battlefield, but NEVER in matters of principle and honor. These two short passages from the pen of a Tennessee farmer, schoolteacher, and junior officer—the first from Burton's letter of April 24 and the second from his letter of April 29—might have come from any of his fellow Confederate soldiers, whether generals or privates:

*"A great gloom overshadows us now. Our fond hopes of independence are all most crushed out. The great cause for which we have been struling for four years to be abandoned and ourselves humiliated. I have nothing to regret. I have been honest in my views and still believe that we were in the right."*

*"As soon as the proper arrangements can be made I expect to take the oath of allegience to the United States and set out home with a clear conscience, having done my duty, stood by the cause for which we have been contending until the last hope is extinguished."*

Burton's next letter was much more optimistic than any one since he received his parole at the first of March. He had finally heard from Anna and knew that things were all right at home, and now he was ready to take the oath and go back to his family. Unfortunately, for him and thousands of other POWs, both Union and Confederate, the war was not quite over yet.

—◊—

*Fort Delaware*
*April 29th 1865*
*My Dear Anna,*

*Your very welcome letter of the 16th inst, was received yesterday, the first since the 1st of March. I have just written to you but had not mailed the letter. I came to the conclusion to stop writing and go in person to see what was the matter and try to get a hearing in that way. So you need not get scared or run away from home should you hear of me some where in the neighborhood prowling around. It may be two weeks, a month, or longer before I get there, so do not get scared to soon. But all jokes aside I expect to come home soon. As soon as the proper arrangements can be made I expect to take the oath of allegience to the United States and set out home with a clear conscience, having done my duty, stood by the cause for which we have been contending until the last hope is extinguished. I will be happy indeed to see and find you all well and pleased to see all my neighbors and friends. You need not write to me any more until you hear from me again. Hoping to see you soon I remain as ever*

*Yours very truly*
*Burton*

—◊—

Even though the fighting was all but finished, there were still several problems to be worked out before the captives could go home.

For the Southern prisoners, things were delayed until Jefferson Davis and the Confederate government were captured and the administration in Washington satisfied itself that President Lincoln's assassination was not a Confederate plot. This took several weeks, so it wasn't until the middle of May that prisoner releases from Fort Delaware began in substantial numbers. As with everything the government does, red tape slowed the process, as well as arranging transportation.

Burton wrote his final letter from prison on May 22nd. It had been two and a half weeks since he had heard from Anna, and he is more frustrated than ever with the delays in being released. Also, he suggests, in a somewhat humorous way, that there will probably be a period of adjustment for both he and Anna when he gets home.

—⁂—

*Fort Delaware*

*May 22nd 1865*

*My Dear Anna*

*I have not heard from you since your letter of the 4th inst. You are probably disappointed in not seeing me by this time. I expected myself to have been home by this time. We are patiently waiting the action of the authorities at Washington for our release. Some are leaving here on special release procured by the influence of friends. Prison life is a greater punishment to me now than ever, But I will try and profit by it as much as possible. I will be able to assist you in the <u>culinary</u> and <u>laundry</u> department, But I have lost four years experience in agriculture and <u>husbandry</u>* [underlining present in the original]. *I have been so long deprived of the society of the gentler sex that I will appear uncouth and a very barbarian when you see me, But you must overlook falts for a while. I expect Lonzo and Dick will be at home soon if they are not alredy there with sad hearts but honor uncompromised. I cannot give you any ideia at what time I will* get home. I can do nothing now but wait. We have a great deal of rain and time seems to move verey slowly. Write to me often it is my greatest consolation. give me all the news. What prospect is there for fruit? Your corn, wheat, garden etc. I feel interested in your garden. I want some vegetables to eat. I think it would make a new man of me to live on vegetables and country air a while. Lee Bullock got a letter from home some time ago stating that some of his friends were endevering to procure his release he has not heard from it since. Give my love to mother. Return my howdy to Kaeiser with a hardy embrace. Believe me as ever

Yours

Burton Warfield


*Author's note:*

This last letter from Burton Warfield is owned by Loreace Concannon, the wife of Burton and Anna's grandson, George Concannon. It was recently discovered and a copy provided to the author by her son, Gary Concannon, and Ted Sahd.

—⁂—

After Burton wrote this last letter, trying to be patient and dreaming of fresh vegetables and country air, it took nineteen more days for him to become a free man. After taking the oath, he was finally released from Fort Delaware on June 10, 1865, four years and five days after going to war, having spent 697 days in four different Yankee prisons.

All over the newly united country, prisoners were being released and beginning to make their way home. Before most of the Southern prisoners were released, the Union forces had already liberated the Confederate prisons, and Union POWs were trying to get home from all over the South. In many cases, those prisoners who felt well enough to fend for themselves simply set off for home on their own, but a great many were provided passage by the government. This proved to be a bonanza of government money for transportation companies who were able to provide the service, but it also opened the door for graft and disaster.

All over the South, groups of recently released Union soldiers were collecting at transportation hubs, anxious to get back home. One such place was the Mississippi River town of Vicksburg. In late April, 1865, the docks were full of steamboats heading upriver, loaded with returning Union soldiers and POWs. The Army was paying $5 a head for passage, and the boat owners were scrambling for a piece of the action. There were also some ugly rumors that a lucrative kickback scheme was operating wherein the steamboat owners would return, under the table, $1 or so of the fare to the army officers in charge to insure that their boat was given a full load.

One of the steamboats docked at Vicksburg on April 24 was the *Sultana*. She had come up from New Orleans, but one of her boilers had begun to leak, so she was delayed at Vicksburg for repairs. Meanwhile, the Union soldiers—and Union money—departed on other boats. Finally, the captain made a deal with the army transportation officers to load his ship as the repairs were being completed. In order to maximize their kickback, the army officers convinced the captain to take a few extra passengers. The *Sultana* was legally registered to carry 376 passengers plus her crew. She pulled away from the dock at Vicksburg late that night with about 2,500 souls onboard, most of them released POWs. To say that it was standing room only was putting it mildly.

Two days later, the *Sultana* docked at Memphis to take on coal, and at midnight, she started upriver again. At 2 a.m. on April 27, about seven miles north of Memphis, the recently repaired boiler exploded, taking two of the remaining three boilers with it. The ship caught fire and drifted back down the river, eventually sinking opposite downtown

Memphis. Between 1,500 and 1,700 passengers drowned, about 1,000 of them recent POWs at the Cahaba prison near Selma, Alabama. The sinking of the *Sultana* remains the worst maritime disaster in United States history, killing as many people as the *Titanic*.[175]

For the Southern prisoners, it was a different situation. When they finally began to be released in substantial numbers in mid-May, the transportation situation was mostly a matter of luck and geography. If a prisoner was being held in the east, like Burton, he might have gotten a train ride to Richmond or some other major rail center, or he might not. If he was in a Midwestern city like Columbus or Indianapolis or Chicago or Rock Island, he was more likely to be let out the front gate and told to get home as best he could. Since almost all the Southern POWs were hundreds of miles from home, surviving AFTER they were released could have been as much a challenge as surviving the prison camp itself.

Two Southern soldiers, John Dyer and Noah Francis, found themselves, after months of enduring miserable conditions, released from Camp Douglas in Chicago, five hundred miles, as the crow flies, from their home near Asheville, North Carolina. There was nothing to do but start walking. Of course, they couldn't walk as the crow flies, so the real distance was much longer. After almost six hundred miles, Francis died and Dyer buried him somewhere in Virginia. John Dyer was one of the lucky ones. He made it home to tell the tale.[176]

Burton's brother-in-law, Samuel Alonzo "Lonny" Worley remained with Burton's old unit until the end of the war and was paroled in North

---

175 Stephen Ambrose, "Remembering Sultana," Online 30 December 2006. *http://news. nationalgeographic.com/news/2001/05/0501_river5.html*.
176 Speer, *Portals to Hell*, 289.

Carolina on May 3. Being a cavalryman, Lonny at least had a horse to ride home. Unfortunately, somewhere near Knoxville, his horse was stolen, so he arrived home on foot, with only the clothes on his back.[177]

We don't know whether Burton Warfield was fortunate enough to get a ride on a Federal train, perhaps all the way to Nashville or even Columbia, or whether he, like so many of his fellow POWs, was forced to make his own way over seven hundred miles back to Maury County. All we know for sure is that Burton was also one of the lucky ones. Sometime in the summer of 1865, he did come home to his wife Anna, his two children, his widowed mother, and his farm near Hampshire, Tennessee, and began to pick up the pieces of his life.

---

177 Story from the Worley family.

CHAPTER THIRTY
## The Move West

*"To the Church at Alma Arkansas or elsewhere"*[178]

*T*he conquered South that Burton traveled through on his way home in the summer of 1865 was a sorry sight. Four years of war had left much of it in ruins. Even relatively quiet areas like western Maury County, Tennessee, couldn't escape the effects. Several significant engagements had been fought within thirty miles of Burton and Anna's farm, and troops of one side or another had passed through on a regular basis.

War had been a constant reality in Middle Tennessee for the last four years. With thousands of troops, both Union and Confederate, operating there, the things we today might refer to as "infrastructure" took a beating. The roads or turnpikes, which held up well enough under the normal traffic before the war had been ground up by uncounted thousands of soldiers' boots, animals' hooves, and wagon and artillery wheels. Bridges over rivers and creeks had been burned by one side and then rebuilt by the other, only to be burned again weeks or months later when the fighting went the other way. Most of the rail fences had long since disappeared, along with the small trees within easy reach, to feed thousands of campfires that boiled coffee and cooked rations for both

---

178 From the letter carried by the Warfield family when they moved to Arkansas. Original from the author's collection.

Johnny Reb and Billy Yank. Miles and miles of railroad had been torn up and the rails heated and bent around trees to prevent their reuse. Thousands of head of cattle and hogs had been rounded up to feed the armies, and the countryside was almost stripped of horses and mules to mount cavalry units and pull wagons and artillery.

Besides the losses mentioned above, there was also the loss in manpower. Farming was still the primary means of making a living for most people, but that was very labor intensive. The slaves, who had supplied a large part of the work force, were now free. Some stayed on their home plantations or farms, working as sharecroppers, but many moved on. Burton Warfield was a small farmer, not a large plantation owner, but he would have needed help for at least part of the year. Before the war, he might have owned a few slaves, or he might have borrowed or rented some from family or friends during planting or harvest time. No longer was that an option.

The loss of the former slaves as a captive labor force was made worse by the toll the war had taken on the white male population. By the end of hostilities, 20 percent of all the adult males in the Southern states had died, and many thousands more had been wounded, crippled, or permanently disabled. In 1865, 20 percent of the State of Mississippi's revenue went to provide artificial limbs for disabled veterans. Five years after the war ended, the total land under cultivation in the South was still five million acres less than the 1860 figure.[179]

Burton and Anna most likely worked their land by themselves at first, taking whatever temporary help they could get, but they had bigger ambitions. Not long after they got home, Burton and his brother-in-law, Lonny Worley, with some help from Anna and Lonny's father, Stephen

---

179 Eric Foner, *Reconstruction*, (New York: Harper and Row, 1988), 125.

Worley, bought a piece of land to farm together. Like the vast majority of veterans, North and South, Burton went about the business of getting reacquainted with his family and neighbors, making a living, and generally trying to survive the chaotic years of reconstruction.

In Tennessee, things were not as bad as in some other places. Having been occupied by Federal forces for most of the war, it had a Loyalist government in place, which was recognized by Washington shortly after Andrew Johnson took over for the assassinated President Lincoln. Because of this, the state avoided some of Reconstruction's worst abuses, but returning Confederate veterans had no voice in the new government. The only people allowed to vote were white males who were "publicly known to have entertained unconditionally Union sentiments." Neither Burton nor his fellow veterans were allowed to vote for five years, until the State Constitution was rewritten in 1870.[180]

In the middle of all this, Burton and Anna went about their business of making a living and raising a family, and except for some tax receipts and brief references in the next two censuses, they drop from the public record for the next seventeen years. There is, however, one surviving letter from this period, showing us that the idea of moving west was being considered soon after the war. Burton and some others actually made a trip to the area around Fort Smith, Arkansas, in the summer of 1869.

—⟋⟍—

*Commercial Hotell*
*Memphis*
*May 7 '69*
*Dear Anna,*

    *We arrived here this evening just about dark. I am now in the third*

---

180 Ibid., 44-45.

story of the Commercial Hotell, as hot as a ginger mill. We got along verry
well thus far. My horse' back is a little sore. We got to Wm. J. Strayhorn's
Wednesday evening and remained there all day Thursday and went
fishing and caught some to. We left there bright and early Friday morning.
I have not seen any of Memphis yet hardly. It is a great place of bustle and
noise. We will cross the river some time tomorrow and then for Arkansas,
mosquitoes, nats, flies, bed bugs, snakes, lizards, wolves, and bears.

Our health is verry good so far. I want to see you and Kaeiser a little
of the worst and haven't been from home but one week. If nothing happens
to prevent we will be at home in seven weeks anyhow. You must write me
at Ft. Smith Ark immediately if you have not already written.

I hope you will all do verry well while I am gone. Uncle Joe is in the
room with me. He says he will not write now but for me to say that he is
verry well with the exception of the Arkansas feaver. I have got well of that.
I believe I will go back and buy in Hardin Co.

Give my regards to all

Yours,

Burton Warfield

—⁓—

Except for the Arkansas adventure spoken of in the above letter, the
Warfield family members are just faces in the crowd in western Maury
County, near the community of Hampshire, until the fall of 1882.
At this point, Burton, now fifty-three years old, decided to move his
family four hundred miles west to Crawford County, Arkansas. Anna
was forty-three. Kaeiser, the little boy who collected chestnuts for his
daddy when he was in Yankee prisons, was now twenty-three and had
evidently gone out on his own. Minnie, the little girl born not long after
Burton went away to war, was twenty-one and now the oldest child still
at home. Since the end of the war, six more children had been born, the

youngest, Annie, less than a year old.

We know that the Warfield family made the trip to Arkansas in the fall of 1882 because of a custom quite prevalent with church members of many denominations during the nineteenth century and continued by some to the present day. When a family moved any distance away, their local church would write them a letter of introduction and recommendation to be presented as their bona fides to their new congregation. The Warfields' local congregation was the Church of Christ at Cathey's Creek, which had been in existence for over fifty years. When they moved to Arkansas, they took with them this letter:

—⁓—

*The church at Cathey's Creek Maury County Tennessee*
*To the church at Alma Arkansas and elsewhere.*

*This will certify that our brother Burton Warfield, his wife Sister N. A. Warfield, and his daughter Sister Minnie Warfield are members in good standing at the church at this place and we commend them to your Christian affection and fellowship.*

*Brother Warfield has served the church here for many years as one of it's chosen elders.*

*By order of the church at Cathey's Creek. October 22nd 1882.*

*P.O. address Isom's Store Maury County Tenn.*

*Thomas J. Brooks*
*Wm. M Cathey Elders*
*A. B. Cathey*[181]

---

181 Original letter in the author's collection. Although it is almost certain that the Warfields moved to Arkansas with seven of their eight children, only the oldest, "Minnie," is mentioned by name in the letter. The church at Cathey's Creek listed only "members" which, to them, meant people old enough to make an informed choice, who then became baptized believers. Since the next oldest child was only sixteen years old, Minnie may have been the only child that fit the definition of "member."

*Burton and Anna Warfield after the move to Arkansas, circa 1885.*
*Original in author's collection.*

—٭—

Their new church at the small community of Alma, Arkansas, was only five years old when Burton, Anna, and Minnie Warfield were added to the church roll as members, numbers 43, 44, and 45, in November 1882.[182]

In western Arkansas, as in Tennessee, farming was the main occupation, so we can assume that Burton took up where he had left off. Among the documents which still exist are several weight slips from local cotton gins showing that he was a regular customer. Another document shows how most of the routine business was conducted in the 1880s and '90s in rural America. There was no bank in the small community of Alma at this time. The closest one was probably in Van Buren, the county seat about fifteen miles away. Truly major transactions might merit the thirty-mile round trip to the bank or the courthouse, but most of the day-to-day business was conducted between individuals or between customers and a small business.

Money was a scarce commodity in small farming communities in the late nineteenth century. Farmers often went months between planting time and harvest with nothing but a few coins to rub together, so everybody had to adapt to the realities of life. The owners of the grocery store or the Feed and Seed, or the doctor or lawyer would keep accounts so that folks could buy on credit until the crop came in. Today, we have a bank or savings and loan on every corner, but back then, most of that business was private. Personal debt instruments would pass between friends, relatives, and business associates as a way to conduct the necessary day-to-day transactions which come with living.

Debt and credit have been a part of society as far back as we have any

---

182 Original record book of the Alma, Arkansas Church of Christ. Author's collection.

records, and Burton Warfield, like most folks back then, found himself on both sides of that equation during his lifetime. Some of his personal records survive, which show him giving his personal pledge to pay a debt, as well as holding notes from others for money owed to him, before, during, and after the Civil War. A small slip of paper giving the amount of the debt and the terms and signed by the party liable for payment was just as binding in Arkansas in the 1880s as a mortgage or credit card bill is today. One document of Burton's that survives today is a good example of how business was done between honest country folks. Shown below is the transcription of Burton's receipt on a slip of plain paper, noting the settlement of a debt he owed to a man named Sam Steward. It even lists the collateral which Burton put up to secure the loan:

*Recd of B. Warfield Fifty-seven & 50/100 in full settlement of note due Nov 20th 1887. Secured by Bill of Sale of one dark brown mare mule aged 7 years - named Liz.*

> *This Nov, 16th 1887.*

> *Sam Steward* (signature)[183]

---

183 Original in the author's collection.

*Burton Warfield receipt for payment of note to Sam Steward,*
*November 16, 1887. Original in author's collection.*

CHAPTER THIRTY-ONE
## Epilog

*"[H]e is a nice old gentleman, worthy of your consideration."*[184]

A t the turn of the century, Burton was seventy-one years old, and he and Anna were living in the Dean's Springs community, Crawford County, Arkansas. In the census of 1900, five children and one grandson are shown as living in the same household with Burton and Anna. At least one other child lived nearby with children of her own. Fourteen years earlier, Mary Burton "Minnie" Warfield had married James A. Farris, a Confederate veteran and a widower in his mid-forties with several children still at home. By now, most of James' children by his first marriage were grown, and he and Minnie had four children of their own: Mattie, the oldest; Ida; Cora; and Hugh.

Minnie Warfield, the daughter of a church elder (Burton had been an elder in Tennessee, and was soon selected as an elder in the church at Alma following the move) obviously brought her faith along to her new family because, soon after the wedding, James Farris became a member of the Alma Church of Christ, followed by several of his children and grandchildren from his first marriage and over the next twenty years, all of his and Minnie's own children.[185]

In March 1903, Burton applied for a Confederate veteran's pension

---

184 Doctor's statement from Burton Warfield's Confederate pension application, 1903
185 Original roll book of the Alma Church of Christ. Author's collection

*Four Generation, circa 1917: from right to left, Anna Worley Warfield,*
*Mary Burton "Minnie" Warfield Farris, Ida Farris Coleman,*
*Billy Coleman (being held) and Farris Coleman (standing).*
*Original in author's collection.*

from the state of Arkansas. He was almost seventy-four years old and not able to farm any more. In that application, he had to furnish proof of his service in the Confederate army, show that he had been a resident of the state for twelve months, owned no more than $400 worth of property, had no more than $150 annual income from all sources, and submit a doctor's statement as to his physical condition. Accordingly, Dr. J. C. Sharp found Burton "totally disabled from performing any manual labor due to hemorrhoids, contracted during his time in the army, kidney trouble and old age." In a wonderful quirk of Victorian bureaucracy, the printed form further required the doctor to state that Burton's disability was "not the result of his own vicious habits still persisted in." To this, the doctor replied "but on the contrary, he is a nice old gentleman, worthy of your consideration."

The pension application was submitted, along with a letter from Tennessee, signed by three former Confederate soldiers attesting to his service, and four months later, Burton Warfield was awarded $75 a year from the state of Arkansas. Seven years later, at age eighty-one, he applied for, and was granted, an increase to $100 a year.[186]

Burton was now one of a dwindling group of Confederate veterans— old men with long white beards who met occasionally to talk about the old days and the "Cause." Burton was active for many years in the Cabell Camp, United Confederate Veterans, in Crawford County, attending the annual reunions held at Farris Grove, a piece of property north of Alma owned by his son-in-law and fellow veteran James Farris, once a private in Company "C," Third Arkansas Cavalry. It was at such reunions that these old soldiers might have talked about experiences and memories they wouldn't discuss with others, even to their closest family members.

---

186 Information from Burton Warfield's pension application. Copy in author's collection

Here were men who would understand.

Burton Warfield, First Lieutenant, Company "A," First Tennessee Cavalry, CSA died on August 10, 1916, at Dean's Springs, Arkansas, aged 87 years, 3 months, and 13 days. Except for Anna, his seventy-seven-year-old widow, there was probably no one at the funeral in the small Church of Christ building where Burton had served for years as an elder, or standing around the new grave at Love Cemetery, a short distance away, who had known him as anything other than a farmer, father, grandfather, and good citizen. In short, what the doctor had said about him thirteen years before—a nice old gentleman.

A turn-of-the-century photograph is the best picture we have of Burton and Anna Warfield. Now owned by their great grandson, Jay Coleman, of Alma, Arkansas, it shows an older couple who look a little stern, as if they aren't enjoying posing for the photographer. There is nothing in the picture to suggest that these people are anything but honest country folks who have spent a hard life working the soil and raising a family. Chances are that even their children didn't really understand the sort of life their parents had once lived. The great Civil War was in the distant past. Only their oldest son had any chance of remembering that time—picking up chestnuts to save for the father he could barely remember. To all the rest, their mother and father had always been farmers—poor but honest Christian folks—the salt of the earth, but nothing noteworthy or heroic. Now that you know their story, however, look at the picture again. It's in the eyes.

We are all captives of the times in which we are born, and Burton and Anna came of age during the most violent, divisive, and bloody time in our country's history. They were part of the generation that endured the firestorm of civil war, and then rebuilt their country into what would become the richest, most powerful nation in recorded

*Burton and Anna Warfield, circa 1900.*
*Original owned by Jay Coleman, Alma, AR.*

history. Now that you know their story, it's possible to see it reflected in that old photograph. In Anna's face is the strength that allowed her, as a twenty-two-year-old wife with two babies, to take over the running of the farm, make the crops so the family could eat and have produce to sell, and care for her widowed mother-in-law—all in enemy-occupied territory—never knowing if her husband, away fighting the war, would live to come home.

In Burton's face, you can still see traces, forty years after the fact, of the man who went off to fight for the "Cause." In his eyes, you can still see the courage and authority of a man who had led other men in battle. There is the officer who once rode with Nathan Bedford Forrest, probably the finest cavalry commander this nation ever produced. There is the soldier who knew the smell of black powder, the sound of minie balls, the sight of blood, and the faces of dead men. In the soldiers' slang of the day, Burton Warfield had "seen the elephant" and not turned back.

Also in the face and the eyes is a different kind of strength. Here is a man who faced both combat and captivity as a soldier. He remained loyal until the war was over, while many others signed the oath rather than endure the life of a POW. He suffered long periods without word from his family or friends, but didn't give up hope. He survived two years of vermin and disease-infested prisons and near-starvation rations, while younger and stronger men died around him. In such extreme conditions, he saw his fellow man at his worst, but also at his best, and kept his faith in God. Most amazing of all, after four years of war, captivity, and, finally, crushing defeat, he was still able to come home and pick up his life.

On that August day in 1916, I hope that some of those people, standing around the new grave in Love Cemetery, knew that they had laid to rest more than just a farmer, a father, a friend, and a Christian gentleman. I hope they knew that he had been a man of courage and endurance during dark times, that he had once fought and suffered for a cause in which he believed passionately.

I hope they knew that Burton Warfield was once a warrior.

*Burton and Anna Warfield's headstone, Love Cemetary,*
*Dean Springs, AR. Photo from author's collection.*

# About the Author

*J*ames R. Knight is a retired Federal Express DC-10 captain, and is also the author of *Bonnie and Clyde: A 21st Century Update*, published in 2003 by Eakin Press, Austin, Texas. He and his wife, Judy, have three children and four grandchildren, and live in Franklin, Tennessee, where he does historical research and volunteers at a local Civil War Historic Site. Mr. Knight was born and raised in Alma, Arkansas, and is the great-great-grandson of James A. Farris, a Civil War veteran and Burton and Anna Warfield's son-in-law.

# Bibliography

PUBLIC DOCUMENTS

Arkansas State Archives. Little Rock, Arkansas. Civil War pension applications of Burton Warfield.

Tennessee State Archives. Nashville, Tennessee. Warfield Official Records. Civil War records of Burton Warfield, including microfilm records of 2nd Battalion, Tennessee Cavalry (Biffle) and 6th Tennessee Cavalry (Wheeler) CSA.

*War of the Rebellion: A Compilation of the Official Records of the Union and Confederate Armies, 1861-1865.* Washington, D.C. 1880-1901. 128 vols.


BOOKS AND ARTICLES

Baumgartner, Richard A. *Blue Lighting.* Huntington, WV: Blue Acorn Press, 1997.

Beitzell, Edwin W. *Point Lookout Prison Camp for Confederates.* Leonardtown, MD: St. Mary's County Historical Society, 1972.

Buell, Thomas B. *The Warrior Generals.* New York: Three Rivers Press, 1997.

Cozzens, Peter. *The Darkest Days of the War*. Chapel Hill and London: University of North Carolina Press, 1997.

Daniel, Larry J. *Shiloh*. New York: Simon & Schuster, 1997.

Dyer, G. W. and J. T. Moore, comp. *The Tennessee Civil War Questionnaires*. Easley, SC: Southern Historical Press.

Fetzer, Dale and Bruce Mowday. *Unlikely Allies: Fort Delaware's Prison Community in the Civil War*. Mechanicsburg, PA: Stackpole Books, 2000.

Foner, Eric. *Reconstruction*. New York: Harper and Row, 1988.

Foote, Shelby. *The Civil War, A Narrative*. Vol. 1. New York: Random House, 1958.

Frohman, Charles E. *Rebels on Lake Erie*. Columbus, OH: Ohio Historical Society, 1965.

Handy, Rev. Isaac. *United States Bonds, Duress by Federal Authorities*. Baltimore: Turnbull Brothers, 1874. Copy supplied by Ft. Delaware Society.

*Historic Maury*. Vol. 5. Columbia, TN: Maury County Historical Society, 1969.

Hurst, Jack. *Nathan Bedford Forrest: A Biography*. New York: Alfred Knopf, 1993.

Joslyn, Maurial P. *Immortal Captives*. Shippensburg, PA: White Mane Publishing Co., 1996.

Lindsley, John Barrien. *Military Annals of Tennessee*. Nashville: J.M. Lindsley & Co., 1886.

Long, Roger. "Johnson's Island Prison." *Blue and Gray*. March, 1987.

McDonough, James Lee and Thomas L. Connelly. *Five Tragic Hours.* Knoxville, TN: University of Tennessee Press, 1983.

Moon, W. H. "Prison Life at Fort Delaware." *Confederate Veteran.* XV. 1907.

Orr, John, Lt. 6th Louisiana. "Prison Experiences." *Confederate Veteran.* XIX, No.1, November 1911.

Perret, Geoffrey. *Ulysses S. Grant, Soldier and President.* New York: Random House, 1997.

Shea, William L. and Earl J. Hess. *Pea Ridge: Civil War Campaign in the West.* Chapel Hill and London: University of North Carolina Press, 1992.

Smith, Frank. *History of Maury County Tennessee.* Columbia, TN: Maury County Historical Society, 1969.

Speer, Lonnie R. *Portals to Hell: Military Prisons of the Civil War.* Mechanicsburg, PA: Stackpole Books, 1997.

Stockdale, Paul H. *Death of an Army.* Murfreesboro, TN: Southern Heritage Press, 1992.

Sword, Wiley. *The Confederacy's Last Hurrah.* Lawrence, KS: University Press of Kansas, 1992.

*Tennesseans in the Civil War.* Part 1. Nashville, TN: Civil War Centennial Commission, 1964.

Watkins, Sam R. *Co. Aytch.* New York: Simon & Schuster, 1st Touchstone edition, 1997.

Welcher, Frank J. and Larry G. Ligget. *Coburn's Brigade.* Carmel, IN: Guild Press of Indiana, 1999.

Welsh, Jack D. *Medical Histories of Confederate Generals.* Kent, OH: The Kent State University Press, 1995.

## LETTERS AND DIARIES—PUBLISHED AND UNPUBLISHED

Alma Arkansas Church of Christ. Original record book. Author's collection.

Bingham, Robert W. Captain, Company "G" 44th NC Infantry. Civil War prison diary. Copy from Rutherford B. Hayes Presidential Center and Library, Spiegel Grove, Fremont, Ohio.

Connolly, James A. *Transactions of the Illinois State Historical Society for the Year 1928*, Springfield: Phillips Bros., 1928. Civil War letters.

Hardison, Capt. W. T. Obituary published in *Confederate Veteran.* Vol. 27, No. 11. November, 1919.

Richardson, J. J. Address to United Confederate Veterans Camp #70. December 17, 1905. Copy from Rutherford B. Hayes Presidential Center and Library, Spiegel Grove, Fremont, Ohio.

Warfield Family Letters. Collection of original letters, currently the property of Jay Coleman, Alma, Arkansas. Additional letters published by *Historic Maury.* Columbia, TN: Maury County Historical Society, 1969.

## WEBSITES

Ambrose, Stephen. "Remembering Sultana." 30 December 2006. *http://news.nationalgeographic.com/news/2001/05/0501_river5.html.*

Sayers, Alethea. "Road to Dishonor." 2004. *http://www.civilwarweb.com.*

# *Acknowledgments*

T hanks are always in order when a task is completed, and although many people helped with this project along the way, I'd like to mention a few who made special contributions.

I had known about these letters for some time, but it was not until my friend, Tricia Westbrooks, became interested in them, took on the grueling job of deciphering the 140-year-old script, and transferred them to a computer, that this project got started. Her work in transcribing and editing the letters made everything else possible.

In order to follow the trail of Burton Warfield and his unit throughout the war, and Burton himself through the Union prisoner of war system, government records were absolutely essential. In this research, the staff and resources of the Tennessee State Archives in Nashville, Tennessee, were lifesavers.

I'd also like to thank Ms. Nan Card and the staff at The Rutherford B. Hayes Presidential Center in Fremont, Ohio, for guiding me through their excellent collection of documents relating to the Johnson's Island Prison. Also, my thanks to Professor David R. Bush of Heidelberg College in Tiffin, Ohio, who allowed me to "walk the ground" of the archaeological dig he and his students were doing on the site of the Johnson's Island prison compound itself. At Fort Delaware State Park, Mr. Daniel Citron and the staff and re-enactors there were a great help.

Above all, I am indebted to my cousin, Jay Coleman, Burton and Anna Warfield's great-grandson, and his family for preserving this record, for allowing me to write the story, and for their friendship and hospitality over the years as I tried to pull all the pieces together.

James R. Knight
Franklin, Tennessee

Printed in the United States
93719LV00002B/169-201/A